CITYSPOTS
NICE

Paul Medbourne

Thomas Cook

Written by Paul Medbourne
Original photography by Paul Medbourne and Patsy Trimnell
Front cover photograph courtesy of Robert Harding, World Imagery

Produced by 183 Books
Design/layout/maps: Chris Lane and Lee Biggadike, Studio 183 Ltd
Editorial/project management: Stephen York

Published by Thomas Cook Publishing
A division of Thomas Cook Tour Operations Limited
PO Box 227, Units 15/16, Coningsby Road
Peterborough PE3 8SB, United Kingdom
email: books@thomascook.com
www.thomascookpublishing.com
+44 (0)1733 416477

First edition © 2006 Thomas Cook Publishing
Text © 2006 Thomas Cook Publishing
Transport map © 2006 Thomas Cook
Other maps © 2006 Thomas Cook Publishing
ISBN-13: 978-1-84157-548-3
ISBN-10: 1-84517-548-8
Head of Thomas Cook Publishing: Chris Young
Project Editor: Kelly Anne Pipes
Production/DTP: Steven Collins

Printed and bound in Spain by GraphyCems

CONTENTS

SYMBOLS & ABBREVIATIONS

The following symbols are used throughout this book:

☎ telephone	⊕ fax	✉ email	�🌐 website address
✉ address	🕐 opening times	Ⓝ public transport connections

The following symbols are used on the maps:

🅸 Tourist Information Office

✈ Airport

CASTEL Beach

Hotels and restaurants are graded by approximate price as follows:
€ Budget €€ Mid-range €€€ Expensive

Abbreviations used in addresses:

av. avenue

blvd boulevard

espl. esplanade

pl. place (square)

prom. promenade

24-HOUR CLOCK

All times in this book are given in the 24-hour clock system used widely in Europe and in most international transport timetables.

 Old and new Nice frame the Baie des Anges

INTRODUCING
Nice

Introduction

The undisputed queen and capital of the French Riviera, Nice is France's fifth largest city, with a permanent population of nearly 400,000 and over ten times that number of visitors annually. Nice-Côte d'Azur airport welcomes more international passengers than any other in France except Paris Charles de Gaulle. Nice began catering to overseas visitors before organised tourism was born and has seen it all, adapting in turn to the tastes of Victorian British aristocracy, *fin de siècle* Russian princes, Jazz Age American millionaires and today's city-breakers, backpackers and family holidaymakers. Tourism is more than Nice's life-blood, it's the city's *raison d'être*.

If there is a 'real' Nice, you are unlikely to find it on a short visit. The ambience is not typically French, nor Italian, even though Nice was an Italian city until 1860 and still retains strong cultural ties to its Mediterranean neighbour. The general standard of food is excellent, and there are plenty of places where you can sample authentic Provençale and French *haute cuisine* at its best, but most of its eating places are geared to international tourist tastes. It enjoys a beautiful setting on the Baie des Anges, but has no sandy beaches of its own. The glamour of the *belle époque* and art deco can still be seen in its buildings, but today it has shed its air of exclusiveness. It has an eventful past and has attracted visits from many of the great names of the last 200 years, and some of its natives, such as Garibaldi, Masséna and Simone Weil, Holocaust survivor and first President of the European Parliament, have been prominent on the world stage, but Nice wears its history lightly.

The truth is that Nice is too laid-back to worry. Its most visible characteristic is a relaxed attitude to life – and it works hard to ensure that its guests are relaxed and entertained. It provides safe and lively streets, seemingly endless sunshine, a clutch of world-class galleries and museums, over 200 hotels, cuisine from all over the world and in every price bracket, vibrant nightlife and an excellent transport infrastructure. Whatever your age, budget or tastes, Nice wants you to enjoy.

△ *Relax by the waterfall of Le Château*

When to go

CLIMATE

For the first hundred years or so of its tourism history, Nice was famed as a winter resort. Its location between the Mediterranean and the sheltering Alpes Maritimes ensures that winter is comparatively warm (average 12°C/53°F December–March, and rarely below 5°C/41°F) and summer not too hot (peaking in July and August at an average 24°C/75°F, though on some days it can reach nearly 30°C/86°F). June and September are probably the best summer months for comfortable heat.

Even better news for the year-round traveller is that even in the darkest winter months you can expect around 5 hours of sunshine a day. On the other hand, all those mountains on the doorstep mean

● Nice's year-round sunshine has been a tourist magnet for 200 years

that the possibility of rain is ever-present (though rarely long-lasting): July is the best travel month for rain-haters, while October and November see the maximum rainfall, around 110mm/4¹/₂ in. average per month (still hardly a deluge).

COSTS

The emergence of no-frills airlines has made Nice, along with many other cities, much more accessible for short breaks. However, the seasonal fare variations can be staggering: a week's return trip on a low-cost airline from a London airport in July will cost around 30% more than the same journey in August, and early spring (except just before Carnaval, see below) can cost a tenth of peak summer. Fares differ sharply also according to the day of the week you choose for your outward and return flight, Wednesday and Thursday generally being a lot cheaper. It pays to investigate thoroughly before choosing dates. Accommodation costs are less variable: as a rule, prices drop only slightly, or not at all, during winter and early spring. Shop around thoroughly through your travel agent or on the web.

ANNUAL EVENTS
February–March

Nice's premier event is the celebrated Carnaval De Nice (see pages 12–13), held in the two weeks preceding Lent and culminating in a grand parade on Shrove Tuesday.

Festin des Cougourdons A traditional festival with local folklore and decorated gourds whose 'interesting shapes', in the words of the official website, 'lend themselves to a wide variety of interpretations'. ❸ Gardens of the Franciscan Monastery, Cimiez.

April
The International Half Marathon of Nice is run along the Promenade des Anglais in late April, along with shorter children's and charity races. Ⓦ www.nicesemimarathon.com

May
La Fête des Mai A traditional family festival held on Sundays and holidays in May. Music, picnics and folk dancing in the gardens and the Amphitheatre of Cimiez.

Nice en Roller International The roller-bladers of Nice's seafront get the chance to compete seriously at the end of the month. Ⓦ www.niceenroller.com

June
Fête de la Mer The fishermen of Nice traditionally celebrate 29 June, the day of their patron St Peter, in this 'Feast of the Sea', with a mass in the Gésu church followed by a procession to the Ponchettes beach in front of the Old Town, where a boat is ceremonially burned.

July–August
Bastille Day 14 July is marked by fireworks on the Promenade des Anglais but there are few other celebrations.

Nice Jazz Festival This big open-air event is held for eight days in July in the atmospheric surroundings of the Arènes de Cimiez (see page 106).

Les Nuits Musicales de Nice, a festival of chamber music, follows on from the Jazz Festival at the end of July and extends for two weeks in early August (see page 106).

La Castellada (mid July–end Aug) Actors and musicians perform the history of the Château (see page 77).

September
Fête de la San Bertoumieu Traditional arts and crafts market held in the Old Town in September in honour of St. Bartholomew.

October
Ste-Réparate Festival Nice celebrates the day of her own patron saint in the Old Town in October with masses, processions, dancing and music.

For a comprehensive list of what's on, see ⓦ www.nicetourism.com

PUBLIC HOLIDAYS
Public transport runs to Sunday schedules, and banks, post offices and public buildings are closed on these days. Many shops (but not generally restaurants) will also be closed.
1 Jan New Year's Day
late Mar/early Apr Easter
8 May Victory Day (World War II)
May/June Whit Sunday, Whit Monday (Pentecost)
14 July Bastille Day
15 Aug Assumption of the Blessed Virgin Mary
1 Nov All Saints Day
11 Nov Remembrance Day
25 Dec Christmas Day

Carnival in Nice

In Nice the traditional pre-Lent celebrations have become an art form and the Riviera's biggest tourist spectacle. The exuberant celebration of Carnaval (from Latin *carne vale*, 'goodbye to meat') was first recorded in 1294. In the 18th century the riotous street parties had given way to exclusive indoor masked balls, and Carnaval was in the doldrums. It took the imagination of local citizen Andriot Saëtone to revive the old carnival spirit and at the same time transform it into one of the greatest shows on earth. His Festival Committee organised the first modern Carnaval parade in 1873, with a presiding monarch, a straw puppet called King Carnaval I. So began the tradition of the Carnaval King, who reigns over the two weeks or more of festivities. In 1876 a Flower Parade along the seafront was added, accompanied by the elegant tossing of bouquets between the carriages of the gentry; this quickly developed into a free-for-all chucking of flower petals into the crowd. These days lads and lasses on each of the 20 floats throw an estimated 100,000 gladioli, roses, carnations and mimosas to the onlookers.

Prominent cartoonists are involved in the design of the theme after which each King is named. The themes are often topical or satirical: 2003's theme was the King of .comMedi@, and 2005 the King of the Deranged Climate. The theme for 2006 is the King of Fools.

The entire festival lasts over two weeks, ending with a grand finale on Shrove Tuesday. On the opening Saturday afternoon King Carnival makes his entrance at the head of 20 themed floats, followed by 180 revellers wearing 'big heads' of papier mâché, accompanied by street theatre and music groups and the first Battle of the Flowers (there are several others during the festival). The programme continues with almost daily processions until the last big afternoon parade, after which, in the evening, King Carnival marches to the beach, where his reign ends as he is ceremonially burnt.

Parades begin on the seafront by the back of the Opera House and march westward along the quai des Etats-Unis and the promenade des Anglais, circling the Jardin Albert 1er and then returning through the main viewing area back along the prom. The north side of the viewing area consists of banks of seating, the south side standing only. Admission to either is by ticket, bought on the day from on-site machines or in advance either online at the Carnaval website, ⓦ www.nicecarnaval.com (up to 48 hours beforehand), or at the tourist office, ⓐ 5 prom. des Anglais. Rates for 2006 vary from €25 per person for a seat at the main opening and closing parades down to €7 for the standing enclosure mid-week.

The 2006 dates are 11–28 February; for a full calendar of events see ⓦ www.nice.fr (navigate to 'Nice Tourisme').

🔺 *Life's one long parade at Carnival time*

History

Greek traders founded Nikaia, 'City of Victory', in the 4th century BC near the modern port, but the area had already been inhabited for hundreds of thousands of years, as the finds displayed at Terra Amata (see page 101) testify. When the Romans arrived in the 1st century BC they preferred to build their settlement, Cemenelum, on the hill which is now the middle-class suburb of Cimiez. The Greek port became the medieval town corresponding to today's Vieille Ville. Possession of the town passed to the Italian House of Savoy, and Italian Nizza only became French Nice in 1860 by the Treaty of Turin. Remnants of the Savoy era include the ruins of the old castle of the Dukes atop the Château hill and the citadel of Villefranche (see page 114).

Nice's harbour was unsuitable for large-scale commerce, and the city might have become a backwater had not 18th-century British travellers discovered its greatest asset – the climate. By 1822 the expat community was large enough to fund the construction of its own seaside walk, the Promenade des Anglais. With the coming of the railway the stream of visitors became a torrent and Queen Victoria's first visit in 1895 bestowed the ultimate seal of approval.

The Russian aristocracy also felt the need to escape their own winters, and by the 1880s were buying and decorating villas, gambling and spending fortunes. Following the Russian Revolution of 1917 Nice was full of suddenly impoverished noblemen. Today's most visible reminder of the Russian invasion is the splendid Orthodox Cathedral (see page 82). Just as Russian money dried up, wealthy Americans discovered the Riviera, and Nice became an expatriate capital of the Jazz Age. *Belle époque* style was succeeded by art deco, best evidenced in the 1927 facade of the Palais de la Méditerranée (see pages 80–81).

Nice's civic reputation in the years after World War II was marred by an unhealthy combination of crime, municipal corruption and ultra-right-wing politics. The return of wealthy Russian visitors, following the fall of the Soviet Union (they are once again the city's top-spending tourist nationality) has brought with it suspicions of Russian Mafia involvement in local crime. Yet this dark side has not prevented Nice from attracting ever-increasing numbers of visitors, further fuelled by the opening of Nice-Cote d'Azur airport in 1954.

LOCAL HEROES

To name a *place*, an *espace*, a *Musée*, a *Lycée* and a *rue* all after one man suggests that the locals must think highly of him. André Masséna was born in Nice in 1758 and after a brief spell in the military settled down in Nice as a shopkeeper with a sideline in smuggling. He re-enlisted after the French Revolution and reached the rank of general at the age of 35, serving under Napoleon as one of France's outstanding commanders until 1811, when his attempt to capture Lisbon was thwarted by the British under the Duke of Wellington. He never again held a command or returned to Nice, dying in Paris in 1817. A brilliant general, a looter on a grand scale and a notorious womaniser, Masséna was rated by his nemesis Wellington as 'the only French commander who gave me sleepless nights'. By contrast, fellow-Niçois Garibaldi is commemorated only in a *place*, a *rue* and a statue. But then, he only reunified Italy, whereas Masséna defended France – although, owing to the changing nationality of Nice, Masséna was born an Italian and Garibaldi a Frenchman!

Lifestyle

By the end of the 19th century Nice was probably the first city in the world whose economy depended on tourism, and catering to the foreign visitor remains its number one business. The result is a truly cosmopolitan and tolerant atmosphere.

If you look at the names in the phone book or at the facades of the buildings in the Vieille Ville you could believe for a moment that you were in Italy. On the other hand, the official infrastructure – police, post offices, Palais de Justice, street names – is totally French, and the iconic images of French life – citizens hurrying by with an armful of fresh *baguettes*, old ladies walking poodles – are in evidence everywhere. But wherever you stroll or sit down in central Nice, the conversations you overhear are as likely to be in English (from both sides of the Atlantic), Russian or Spanish as in French.

Perhaps it's harder to spot the residents because they enjoy much the same lifestyle as the tourists, and they have the leisure to do it – 11 per cent of the city's population are students, 27 per cent are retired people. Visitors and natives seem to share the same basic pleasures – eating, drinking, chatting, promenading, people-watching and window-shopping. So it's not difficult to fit in, just enjoy yourself.

Having said that, life is just that bit easier if you observe some of the local niceties. Don't forget to say *bonjour* to the shopkeeper and *au revoir* when you leave the shop; include a *s'il vous plaît* when you ask for something and a *merci* when you receive it. Call the waiter *monsieur*. Begin a conversation with your hotel receptionist or bus driver with a few words of French, however bad; once local honour has been satisfied, you will soon find the conversation turns into English.

● *Hanging out, strolling, eating and drinking are major occupations*

Culture

Whether it's due to the wealth and refined tastes of its upmarket 19th-century visitors or the magnetism that the Côte d'Azur has always exerted on artists, or maybe in an attempt to demonstrate that it's more than just a great holiday resort, Nice offers an amazing number of top-class public art galleries and museums in and around the city. If you're serious about art (particularly if 20th-century art is your thing) you could easily fill an affordable and rewarding trip of four or more days in Nice in the low season just taking them all in, with the bonus of all that winter sunshine and seaside air in between visits. A pass giving unlimited access for any 7 days within a period of 15 days to all of Nice's municipal galleries and museums (which do not include the Chagall and Asiatic Art museums) can be purchased at any of them, price €6. In any case, admission to all the municipal museums is free on the first and third Sundays of each month.

The cream of the 20th-century selection includes the Musée Matisse in the Cimiez district (see page 100), the Musée National Message Biblique Marc Chagall just north of the city centre (see page 99), MAMAC (Musée d'Art Moderne et d'Art Contemporain) near the old town, featuring a wide selection of international modern art (see page 98). Further afield the Fondation Maeght at St-Paul-de-Vence (see page 135) is a treasure-house of over 6000 works by Braque, Chagall, Léger, Kandinsky, Miró and others, and the Musée Renoir at Cagnes preserves the artist's studio. More wide-ranging collections are housed in the Musée des Beaux-Arts Jules-Chéret (see page 84), with priceless works of the 15th–20th

● *Musée Matisse is one of Nice's cultural highlights*

centuries, and the Musée Masséna (if it ever re-opens – see page 80), both to the west of the city centre.

Those with an interest in history and archaeology will want to see the Roman-era discoveries in the Musée d'Archéologique in Cimiez and the nearby Arènes (see pages 97, 99), the prehistoric finds and reconstructions at Terra Amata (see page 101), and – when it finally reopens – the history of the city catalogued in the Musée Masséna. More specialist and farther out of town, but well worth a visit for the quality of its collections of oriental exhibits, is the Musée des Arts Asiatiques (see page 84).

The other main aspect of Nice's cultural life is music. Aside from the Jazz Festival and Nuits Musicales (see page 106), the summer months are rich in musical events, many of them free: June has its sacred music recitals in churches around the town, and in July a series of free concerts of Mediterranean and world music, under the collective name **Musicalia**, takes place at the open-air Théâtre de Verdure near the seafront on Wednesday and Saturday evenings. The same venue sees performances of opera and operetta in September, as does the Opéra de Nice (see page 76). The What's On section of the Nice Tourism site (ⓦ www.nicetourism.com) gives listings and offers an on-line booking service for musical events.

● *Browse for bargains in the narrow streets of the Old Town*

Shopping

SHOPPING AREAS & MARKETS

The few large department stores in Nice are found along av. Jean Médecin, including the unmissable ochre facade of Galeries Lafayette, a branch of the renowned Parisian store, and two blocks further up the Etoile shopping mall, four storeys of chain store fashion shops, cafés, FNAC and a large branch of C&A. The avenue also sports a wide range of smaller fashion boutiques and businesses selling bags and leatherware. Note: the construction of the new tramway (see page 57) has ripped up large parts of the avenue and surrounding streets, causing maximum inconvenience to pedestrians, and this will probably continue for most of 2006.

The long, busy pedestrianised zone of the rue de France and rue Masséna, heading west from the top of place Masséna, is a bustling thoroughfare of small souvenir shops and individual fashion boutiques. Famous designer names congregate just to the south and west of the place Masséna, near the Jardin Albert 1er.

As well as containing the city's most enticing markets (see below), the old town is crowded with small shops. Many of them are true specialists in everything from faïence and mosaics to hand-made toiletries, chocolates and foodstuffs, others offer a general range of souvenirs aimed unashamedly at the tourist purse.

The markets in the cours Saleya in the Vieille Ville are great places to browse. In the daily Flower Market (see page 64) you can pick up dried flowers, enticing packs of herbs and spices and craft items, as well as improbably coloured candy and sweets and top-quality fresh produce for a picnic. The night market in the same

● *Cours Soleya is an antique hunter's paradise*

location offers a wide range of gift ideas, from the funky to the irresistibly tacky. On Mondays the market changes to *brocante* (bric-a-brac); goods on sale range from exquisite vases to battered but authentic gendarme's caps (as well as a lot of absolute junk).

BEST BUYS & LOCAL SPECIALITIES

There are no heart-stopping bargains in Nice but, equally, commerce is too competitive to allow rip-off prices. Generally the quality is good for the price, and in some categories the quality can be very good indeed. Nice's proximity to the perfumeries of Grasse and herb-growing areas of Provence ensures a wide offering of hand-made perfumes, soaps and toiletries. Dried and fresh herbs themselves are available in profusion and make good gifts. Olives and olive oil are another regional speciality and Nice offers a tempting choice at a quality unmatched elsewhere on the Med. Colourful Provençal fabrics are sold everywhere, either by the length or made up as table linen or clothing. If you are seriously interested in antiques, the shops of the Quartier des Antiquaires (see page 72) are worth checking out, in addition to the Monday market in the cours Saleya (see above). Don't overlook the shops attached to public galleries, museums and attractions; you can pick up excellent reproduction prints, as well as books and art-decorated tableware, at reasonable prices.

FOOD & EVERYDAY SHOPPING

As in most French cities, you are never far from a small grocer's shop or *boulangerie* (baker's), and of course the markets offer superb produce. If you need to buy a range of everyday necessities it makes sense to use one of the small supermarkets – look for the names Monoprix (central, on av. Jean Médecin), Casino and Intermarché (outlets along the blvd Gambetta on the western edge of the city centre). If you are travelling by car, the 140 stores of the Cap 3000 complex at St-Laurent-du-Var near the airport will supply your every shopping need.

○ *Printed Provençal fabrics make great take-home gifts*

USEFUL SHOPPING PHRASES

What time do the shops open/close?
A quelle heure ouvrent/ferment les magasins?
Ah kehlur oovr/fehrm leh mahgazhang?

How much is this?
C'est combien?
Cey combyahng?

Can I try this on?
Puis-je essayer ceci?
Pweezh ehssayeh cerssee?

My size is ...
Ma taille (clothes)/
ma pointure (shoes) est ...
Mah tie/mah pooahngtewr ay ...

I'll take this one, thank you
Je prends celui-ci/celle-ci merci
Zher prahng serlweesi/sehlsee mehrsee

Eating & drinking

WHERE TO GO

You will never have trouble in finding somewhere to eat in Nice.
Even in late evening on Bastille Day you would be unlucky to have to
walk more than a few yards before finding a free table for two.
Budget is not a limitation, either. Nice caters equally well for cheap
snacks and gourmet dining, with an endless mass of mid-range
eateries in between that all offer a uniform but reliable bill of fare –
excellent pizzas, standard pasta and Italian dishes, *moules frites*
(steamed mussels and french fries) and seafood. Restaurants cluster
around the main foci of tourist traffic: the rue de France/rue
Masséna pedestrian zone, the Vieille Ville, the seafront and the area
round the rail station. Don't overlook the port area, which is lined
with excellent seafood restaurants and some lively bars. Oriental
and Asian cuisine is well catered for in most of these areas, and
Turkish and Middle Eastern establishments are not hard to find.
Specifically vegetarian restaurants are few, but it's easy to find tasty
meat- and fish-free pizzas and salads on any menu; higher-class

RESTAURANT CATEGORIES

In this book the approximate price bands into which
restaurants fall are based on the average cost of a
three-course evening meal for one person, excluding drinks,
indicated by these symbols:
€€€ Over €50; **€€** €16–50; **€** €15 or under.
Bear in mind that a one-course lunch in a **€€€** establishment
may well be at a **€€** cost, and so on.

◆ *Many pizzerias stay open until the small hours*

establishments will nearly always offer vegetarian choices.

Choosing a restaurant a few minutes' walk away from the most crowded streets will usually knock a few euros off the bill, though the ambience may not be so vibrant. Seafood, plentiful and top-quality everywhere, is generally more expensive than meat-based dishes. The higher-range restaurants tend to close earlier, by 22.30 or 23.00, but the mid-range pizza/pasta eateries in the main tourist locations will still be serving (and still crowded) well after midnight.

A regular-sized beer will set you back about €3, more if the bar or café is upmarket enough to set out a few complimentary olives and peanuts with your glass. On the other hand, you can make one drink last all night without getting a sour look from the waiter – drinking is regarded as an accompaniment to conversation, not an end in itself. If cocktails are your tipple, use the bar of a smart hotel; the versions served in ordinary cafés can be poor imitations. Most restaurants will offer a selection of mainly French wines; the climate and cuisine are tailor-made for a chilled bottle or carafe of rosé, in which the local Provençal and Corsican vineyards excel.

Restaurant menus are usually *service compris* – unless you have had really good service in a more upmarket restaurant, there's no need to tip. At most, you might leave the small change behind after a drink in a café. The major credit cards are accepted everywhere for all but the cheapest meals. Although by law all French restaurants should have a non-smoking area (*Espace non-fumeur*) it may be hard to find and even then not very well observed.

FAST FOOD, LIGHT MEALS, PICNICS & SELF-CATERING
Nice has its own native fast-food options in *socca*, *pan bagnat* and *pissaladière* (see overleaf), and you shouldn't leave without trying them. Take-away food in the shape of sandwiches, filled rolls, pizza slices and kebabs is ubiquitous. If you can't get through a holiday without a McDonalds, you'll find the golden arches at 1 prom. des Anglais, another at the bus station and a third on av. Jean Médecin.

Nice is picnic heaven – fresh bread (and tempting pastries) from the *boulangerie*, cooked meats and cheese from the *charcuterie* and superb salads and fruit from the greengrocers, or better still the morning market in the cours Saleya. On blvd Jean Jaurès, opposite the bus station, is a trio of these three where you can collect all the elements of a gourmet picnic in five minutes, with only another 5-minute walk to the green spaces of the Château hill.

◗ *Everything for a picnic, for sale at the boulangerie*

⬢ *Salade niçoise with all the trimmings*

LOCAL SPECIALITIES

Nice's best known dish is *salade niçoise*, a delicious summer option of tuna, eggs, anchovies, beans and salad – the better the restaurant the more elaborate the version. Served up in a roll as fast food it becomes *pan bagnat*. *Socca* is a simple snack, a pancake of chickpeas flour, garlic and oil. *Pissaladière* is a thin pizza-like snack topped with fried onions, anchovies and olives (no cheese or tomato). If you want to try *bouillabaisse*, the south coast's traditional meal-sized fish stew, you'll need to select a restaurant that does it and then usually give at least 24 hours' notice.

USEFUL DINING PHRASES

I would like a table for ... people
Je voudrais une table pour ... personnes
Zher voodray ewn tabl poor ... pehrson

Waiter/waitress!
Monsieur/Mademoiselle,
s'il vous plaît!
M'sewr/madmwahzel,
sylvooplay!

May I have the bill, please?
L'addition, s'il vous plaît!
Laddyssyawng, sylvooplay!

Could I have it well-cooked/medium/rare please?
Je le voudrais bien cuit/à point/ saignant
Zher ler voodray beeang kwee/ah pwang/saynyang

I am a vegetarian. Does this contain meat?
Je suis végétarien (végétarienne). Est-ce que ce plat contient de la viande?
Zher swee vehzhehtarianhg (vehzhehtarien). Essker ser plah kontyang der lah veeahngd?

Where is the toilet (restroom) please?
Où sont les toilettes, s'il vous plaît?
Oo sawng leh twahlaitt, sylvooplay?

Entertainment & nightlife

Nice's climate encourages open-air amusement. Enjoying a leisurely outdoor meal, relaxing with a drink or two, enjoying one of the open-air musical events such as the Jazz Festival or Musicalia (see page 20), taking in the night views over the Baie des Anges, the bustle of promenaders on the seafront, the antics of street performers and the strains of the (mainly East European) street

○ No one goes to bed early in Nice

musicians – for most visitors this is enough to fill an evening. However, the city offers plenty of more active options.

CASINOS

If you're over 21 and can afford to lose a few euros, a casino provides great evening entertainment. Dress smartly to get past the doormen and take your passport with you for ID and then, after maybe playing a few of the slots, move on to the tables, for which there will be a small admission charge. You don't have to bet your shirt to enjoy the experience – the real entertainment is in watching the high rollers and rubbing shoulders with the Riviera's rich and (sometimes) famous. The serious action doesn't start until around 22.00, but you can pass the time in the bar or restaurant. Nice's two casinos, Casino Ruhl and Palais de la Méditerranée, are both on the promenade des Anglais (see page 90).

CINEMA

You can catch movies in English (with French subtitles) at these cinemas:

Rialto ⓐ 4 rue de Rivoli.
Le Nouveau Mercury ⓐ 16 pl. Garibaldi.
Cinémathèque de Nice (see page 97) ⓐ 3 espl. Kennedy.

CLUBS, DISCOS & LIVE MUSIC

If your night isn't complete without dancing, there are plenty of discos and bars with dancing. The choice runs from discos to piano bars and pubs and cafés with live music (and in some cases karaoke nights). Streets running off the seafront, the old town and the port area are the best areas to check out. For an exhaustive list, see ⓦ www.nicetourism.com or the media listed on page 152.

Sport & relaxation

BEACH & WATERSPORTS

There are 14 public beaches along the Baie des Anges, as well as the stretches reserved for guests of hotels. All of them are pebble beaches, which doesn't put off the thousands of sun-worshippers who make for them every day. Those which lay on a children's play area include Bambou, Forum, Lido, Miami, Neptune, Ruhl and Voilier. Bambou, Florida and Neptune also have pedalos for hire. If you like sand with your sea, take a short trip to neighbouring Villefranche-sur-Mer (see page 112) for a family-style beach or Beaulieu-sur-Mer (see page 116) for a more sedate sort of resort.

Swimming is okay anywhere; the beaches get high EU ratings and are supervised by lifeguards and the water reaches a very warm 25°C/77°F in summer. You'll be able to find opportunities to pursue a wide variety of watersports on Nice's beaches:

Jet Ski: Beau Rivage, Florida, Forum and Sporting.
Parascending: Blue, Forum, Neptune, Opera and Ruhl
Windsurfing: Neptune and Opera.
Scuba diving: Nice is where much of today's standard scuba equipment was invented, by the Forjon family between the wars; the Centre International de Plongée de Nice offers a first-time for beginners (called a *baptême*) and

🔘 *Birds-eye view of the Med*

packages for more experienced divers. ⓐ 2 ruelle des Moulins (near the quai des Docks on the east of the old port), ⓣ 04 93 55 59 50. Villefranche is another good centre for diving of all kinds.

OTHER OUTDOOR ACTIVITIES

There are plenty of companies offering activities such as riding, golf and hiking, but they will all involve going some way out of town. The Tourist Office (see page 151) will be happy to help you, and you can preview the range of opportunities at ⓦ www.nicetourisme.com However, you don't have to go very far to enjoy walking. The hill of Le Château (see page 67) is perfect for a gentle stroll in the fresh air. For a longer and more invigorating walk catch a bus to the hillside of Mont Boron (see page 94).

SPORT

Nice's football (soccer) team plays at the 18,000-seater Stade du Ray in the northern suburbs (ⓝ Bus 18 from the city centre). OGC Nice may not have the international presence of Riviera neighbours AS Monaco, but in the 2004/5 season they managed a respectable 12th place in the French First Division. The French football season runs from August to May and weekend matches are played on Saturdays – check out the local press. Crowds are small (12,000 for the local derby with Monaco) but the supporters' Gallic passion makes for a great atmosphere, and tickets are much cheaper than for English Premiership games.

If you want to try your hand at a more typically French sport, you can play boules (pétanque) on the beaches in Nice; at St-Paul-de-Vence (see page 135) the local tourist office will sell you a package of 2 hours of instruction. If you want to see the game played by experts, Nice hosts the Europétanque d'Azur championships each July around the Jardin Albert 1er, in which over 500 local teams participate.

Accommodation

With over 12,000 hotel beds and more than 700 holiday apartments on offer, plus a good selection of youth hostels, Nice has no shortage of accommodation, though much of it is at the more expensive end of the market. The cheapest hotels cluster around the main rail station, which entails a bus ride or a 20 minute walk to the sea and the old town; mid-price options are mainly located in the central boulevards, a reasonable walk from the seafront, shops and sights. The central seafront and its side-streets are mostly the preserve of luxury hotels. If you are travelling by car, you also have the option of a reasonably priced motel room near the airport. Whatever accommodation you have in mind, remember that the French take their summer holidays in late July and August: book well in advance for that period.

HOTELS

Unless you have booked an inclusive package, it pays to investigate thoroughly on the web; in addition to the many commercial sites, the tourist office offers listings and instant reservations at ⓦ www.niceres.com, which also covers self-catering. Listed below are a few recommendations, but there are many more good hotels to choose from. The ratings indicate average price per double room per night – some rooms may be more or less expensive than the rating suggests:

PRICE RATING
€€€ Upwards of €200; €€ €100–200; € Under €100.

Breakfast is always extra and often poor value; some hotels lay on a full buffet, others the bare minimum of coffee, juice and rolls. If your hotel is one of the latter, take your *petit déjeuner* at any pavement café (many of which also do an 'English' or 'American' breakfast).

Meyerbeer Beach € Small hotel close to the western end of the seafront and the pedestrianised centre, with 16 well equipped rooms and free internet access. ⓐ 15 rue Meyerbeer. ⓣ 04 93 88 95 65.

Albert 1er €–€€ 1930s building on the edge of the Vieille Ville, with great views of the city and the bay. 72 sound-proofed rooms with charming oak furniture. ⓐ 4 av. des Phocéens. ⓣ 04 93 85 74 01; ⓦ www.hotel-albert-1er.fr

Campanile Centre Acropolis €–€€ Usually the motels of this chain are on city outskirts, but this one is very central, a few blocks from the bus station and within walking distance of the Vieille Ville. Basic but clean and breakfast buffets are good. There is another Campanile near the airport. ⓐ 58 blvd Risso. ⓣ 04 93 26 20 60; ⓦ www.campanile.com

Suisse €€ A neighbour of La Pérouse and sharing all the advantages of its location, but at a lower price. Great sea views from many of its 42 rooms. ⓐ 15 quai Rauba Capeu. ⓣ 04 92 17 39 00.

Villa Victoria €€ Central quiet location and helpful staff, with a shady garden for relaxation. ⓐ 33 blvd Victor Hugo. ⓣ 93 88 39 60; ⓦ www.villa-victoria.com

🔺 *Many 19th-century town houses have been converted to hotels such as the Villa Victoria*

Windsor €€ Stylish and different without costing a fortune. Many of the rooms have been individually decorated by leading modern artists; on-site services include massage, sauna and Turkish bath. ⓐ 11 rue Dalpozzo. ⓣ 04 93 88 59 35; Ⓦ www.hotelwindsornice.com

Beau Rivage €€–€€€ Recently renovated classic hotel, once the home of Matisse, in the heart of the old town but backing onto the seafront, with 118 rooms and a private beach. ⓐ 24 rue St-François-de-Paule. ⓣ 04 92 47 82 82; Ⓦ www.hotel-beau-rivage-nice.cote.azur.fr

Negresco €€€ A Nice landmark since 1912 and the grand old lady of the Riviera, patronised over the years by the elite of Nice's visitors. 121 rooms and 24 suites, all individually decorated. The restaurant, Le Chantecler, is Michelin-starred (of course). ⓐ 37 prom. des Anglais. ⓣ 04 93 16 64 00; Ⓦ www.hotel-negresco-nice.com

Palais de la Méditerranée €€€ The modern hotel and casino behind the 1930 art deco facade of its predecessor was built by the Taittinger champagne dynasty and opened in 2000. ❷ 15 prom. des Anglais. ❶ 04 92 14 77 00; ❺ www.concorde-hotels.com

La Pérouse €€€ Set into the cliffside of the Château hill at the eastern end of the Baie des Anges and well placed for the Vieille Ville and the port. ❷ 11 quai Rauba-Capeau. ❶ 04 93 62 34 63; ❺ www.hroy.com/la-perouse

SELF-CATERING

For stays of a week or more, especially if travelling as a family, consider renting a holiday apartment; many of the complexes are modern and very central, and the abundance of food outlets and markets makes self-catering easy. Prices are comparable with inexpensive–mid-range hotels. Check out the Nice tourism website (❺ www.nicetourisme.com) for the options.

YOUTH HOSTELS

Auberge de Jeunesse (HI) € The cheapest option, but on a hillside 4 km/2½ miles out of town. ❷ rte Forestière du Mont Alban. ❶ 04 93 89 23 64. ❸ all year. ❹ Buses 14, 82: Route Forestière.

Espace Magnan € About 1 km/¾ mile west of the centre and close to the sea, with plenty of bus connections. ❷ rue Louis Coppet. ❶ 04 93 86 28 75. ❸ all year for groups, Jun–Sept for individual bookers.

Forum Nice-Nord € In the northern suburbs, about 2km/¾ mile out from the centre. ❷ 10 blvd Comte de Falicon, ❶ 04 93 84 24 3. ❸ all year, groups only. ❹ Bus 18: Comte de Falicon.

Résidence Internationale La Maison Blanche € Welcomes foreign students and within walking distance of the old town.
🅐 14 blvd Carabacel. ☎ 04 93 62 15 70; 🌐 www.residazur.com

THE NEGRESCO

Henri Negresco, Romanian-born director of the Monte Carlo Casino, decided he could trade on his excellent contacts with royalty and millionaires by creating the grandest hotel on the Riviera, a palace fit to house his superstar friends. The result was the 1912 pink and white confection by Eduoard Niermans that has become a National Historic Building and an icon of Nice. The interior has a fabulous art collection, with some quirky touches, such as the carousel in the lobby and the gloriously tacky illuminated name sign outside. Unlike many of the world's big-name hotels, it is still privately owned and run.

CAMPING

The Nice tourist office lists some 21 campsites (There are none in Nice itself; the nearest location being Cagnes-sur-Mer, about 20 km from the centre of Nice via the A8 motorway. 🚌 30 mins by bus TAM 200, 400, 500, Lignes d'Azur 94 or less than 20 mins by train (bear in mind that the campsite may be some way from the bus stops and rail station in the middle of Cagnes). Other possibilities, a little further out, are Villeneuve-Loubet and Antibes.

🔘 *The grand old lady has become a Nice landmark*

THE BEST OF NICE

You can do and see a lot in Nice in a few days, though if you are an art-lover, or plan to explore the Riviera from your city base, you could easily spend a couple of weeks without repeating anything. If time is limited, don't rule out a ride on the little white tourist 'train', or the more wide-ranging open-top bus tour, as a way of sampling the top sights of Nice. Both depart from the southern side of the prom. des Anglais, facing the Jardin Albert 1er.

Petit Train Touristique 40-minute tour, with commentary, of the old town and the Château hill. Fare €6, half-price for children under 9. Ⓦ www.petittrainnice.com Ⓛ Daily 10.00–19.00; departures every 30 mins.

Le Grand Tour open-top bus Tours last about 2 hours and take in Cimiez to the north and Mont Boron in the east. Tickets available on the bus or from the tourist offices. Fare €17, reductions for children and seniors. Ⓣ 04 92 29 17 00. Ⓛ Daily 09.30–18.50 (last tour of the day, which is cheaper).

For the best attractions for children, see pages 147–149.

TOP 10 ATTRACTIONS

- **Vieille Ville** Exploring the colourful streets and markets (see page 62).

- **Cathédrale Orthodoxe Russe St-Nicolas** The architecture and atmosphere of the Russian cathedral (see page 82).

- **Promenades** A summer evening stroll along the promenade des Anglais and quai des Etats-Unis. You're guaranteed a couple of hours of free entertainment.

- **A meal in the Cours Saleya** A leisurely outdoor dinner anywhere in the cours (see page 64) – enjoy the food and the buzz around you.

- **Musée Chagall** Chagall's enigmatic masterpieces in Cimiez (see page 99).

- **A walk around the Château hill** to cool off and admire the views of the old town and port (see page 67). Collect your picnic ingredients in the market on the way there.

- **The Riviera** A day-trip to any of destinations listed on pages 108–110.

- **Open-air music** Jazz or classical music at the Arènes de Cimiez (see page 106) or one of the free concerts of the Musicalia (page 20).

- **Lunch at the Negresco** A spoil-yourself treat at the Michelin-starred brasserie (see page 38).

- **The Port by night** Soaking up the lively atmosphere or dancing the night away in one of the quayside bars.

🔽 *Nice's bustling Port de Plaisance*

Here's a quick guide to seeing the best of Nice, depending on the time you have available.

HALF-DAY: NICE IN A HURRY

If you're just calling into Nice on a longer Riviera holiday, or maybe catching some sightseeing during a business trip, concentrate on the Vieille Ville (page 62). Try to make it a morning, so that you can experience the Flower Market in the cours Saleya (not Mon) before heading up the side streets and reaching the pl. Rossetti for a visit to the cathedral and a well-earned drink or ice cream at Fenocchio's. Don't miss the House of Adam and Eve, the Chapelle Ste-Rita or the Palais Lascaris on the way.

1 DAY: TIME TO SEE A LITTLE MORE

If you have the afternoon and early evening as well, leave the old town at the Ponchettes exit from cours Saleya and take a walk along the seafront, beginning, along the quai des Etats-Unis and continuing along the prom. des Anglais as far as the Hotel Negresco. You could use some of the time to soak up the sun on the beach, or head up from the promenade into the pedestrian-only rue Masséna for some retail therapy or a meal at one of the area's excellent pizza and pasta restaurants.

2–3 DAYS: SHORT CITY-BREAK

After the above whistle-stop tour of the centre, chill out the next day with a morning stroll on the Château hill and descend from there into the port to marvel at the opulent yachts and enjoy some freshly caught seafood. From the port it's not a long walk to MAMAC (see page 98) and its quirky pop-art collection. Use your remaining time for short bus rides to Cimiez for the Chagall and Matisse museums, the Roman remains and the Franciscan monastery (see pages 96–97), to the Russian Orthodox cathedral in the north-west of the town (see page 82), and a little further afield, to the Beaux-Arts or Asiatic Art museums (both page 84).

LONGER: ENJOYING NICE TO THE FULL

You'll want to return to some of the places suggested in the 2–3 day schedule, by day and night, but a longer visit gives you time to explore along the Riviera, which is easy with the excellent train and bus services. Make Villefranche (page 112) and St-Paul-de-Vence (page 132) your top priorities.

❥ *You can catch the flower market on any day except Monday*

Something for nothing

You don't have to put your credit card into the red to enjoy Nice, and many of its best experiences come at little or no charge. A cup of coffee at an outside table may seem a little pricey in itself, but it buys you a seat all morning if you want, while passing performance artists, locals and tourists keep you constantly entertained. Sunshine, fabulous views and fresh air are free, and there's nowhere better to enjoy them than the Château park (see page 67). If you get a little hot, stand close to the waterfall and let it spray you cool.

It costs nothing to walk along the seafront, either, on any summer evening and take in the street life – from seriously competitive rollerbladers to African drumming groups – that the promenade and the beach attract like magnets. In fact, anywhere in central Nice is good for people-watching, especially the markets. Buying a pair of antique vases at the Monday morning market in the cours Saleya can take *madame* up to half-an-hour before she and the stallholder are satisfied the price is right, and the entire gamut of human emotion and Gallic gesture will be displayed in the process.

Remember that all the municipal museums (not the Chagall or Asiatic Art museums, sadly) have free entrance on the first and third Sundays of each month. Other must-see sights which are permanently free of charge include the cathedral and the Palais Lascaris (both page 66). You can enjoy Musicalia, free concerts of Mediterranean and world music, at the open-air Théâtre de Verdure (between the seafront and the Jardin Albert 1er) Wednesday and Saturday evenings in July.

▶ *People watching all morning for the price of a cup of coffee*

When it rains

You would be unlucky, even in winter, to be forced indoors by rain in Nice for more than a morning, but for days when even the Mediterranean looks grey, the city offers all kinds of escapes.

With over 60 museums and galleries in the vicinity, not to mention villas, churches and palaces, there's always somewhere to while away a few hours indoors. The star museums – Musée Chagall, Musée Matisse, MAMAC, the Beaux-Arts and Asiatic Arts museums – could all easily occupy a half day. If you're a cinema buff you'll love the Cinemathèque's performances of old classics in all languages (see page 97). Bad weather can't spoil the indoor attractions of the of the old town, either – its baroque churches, the cathedral, the Palais Lascaris – and it also provides the perfect opportunity to gaze at the bejewelled interior of the Russian Orthodox Cathedral.

As well as cultural attractions, the temples of commerce offer a very handy refuge from the weather. Browsing in the Galeries Lafayette or the Etoile shopping mall on av. Jean Médecin could keep shopaholics happily occupied for an entire day, including a spot of lunch. Smaller shops also have more to offer than you think – several of the mosaics boutiques in the Vieille Ville invite you to try your hand at this fascinating handicraft. In the same area, Poterie Painting (see page 70) will show you how to create your own souvenirs by designing and painting your own pottery to take away with you. If you are looking for something more active, why not get wet anyway, in one of Nice's *piscines* (indoor swimming pools)? The two most central are:

Piscine Jean Médecin ⓐ 178 rue de France. ⓣ 04 93 86 24 01.
Piscine St-François ⓐ 13 pl. St-François. ⓣ 04 93 85 53 08.

● *Browsing in galleries is a great way to escape the rain*

On arrival

TIME DIFFERENCES

French clocks follow Central European Time (CET). During Daylight Saving Time (end Mar–end Oct), the clocks are put ahead 1 hour. In the French summer, at 12.00 noon, time at home is as follows:

Australia Eastern Standard Time 20.00, Central Standard Time 19.30, Western Standard Time 18.00

New Zealand 22.00

South Africa 12.00.

UK and Republic of Ireland 11.00

USA and Canada Newfoundland Time 07.30, Atlantic Canada Time 07.00, Eastern Time 06.00, Central Time 05.00, Mountain Time 04.00, Pacific Time 03.00, Alaska 02.00.

ARRIVING

By air

The descent to Nice by air is an experience in itself. The runways are almost surrounded by the sea, and as the plane descends you get some wonderful views of the Côte d'Azur. The airport is the second largest in France in terms of passengers (8 million a year) but it's a manageable size and gets its customers landside pretty quickly. In each of the two terminals there are two banks to take care of any foreign exchange needs, ● 08.00–22.00 all year. The airport isn't a long way from the city. Buses run from outside Terminal 1 every half-hour: nos 98 and 99 to the centre, no. 23 through the western edge of the city centre to Nice-Ville rail station – about a 30-minute journey in all cases, fare under €2. If you prefer to take a taxi, the journey time's about the same and the fare around €25. For the same price you can pre-book a door-to-door

⬆ *The views start before you even land*

minibus, better value if there are 5–8 people in your party, from
Ⓦ www.a-t-s.net. The local TER train will get you to Nice-Ville station in
about 20 minutes, but it's a 500-yard walk from the terminal to St
Augustin, the airport station. Car hire firms at the airport include ADA,
Avis, Budget, Europcar, Hertz, National/Alamo and Sixt; the pick-up
point is outside Terminal 2 (reached from Terminal 1 via free shuttle
bus).

Nice-Côte d'Azur Airport ❶ flight information 0820 423 333;
Ⓦ www.nice.aeroport.fr

By rail

The main SNCF rail station, Nice-Ville, is situated on the northern edge
of the city centre, and is served by many buses (no. 4 offers the most
direct route to central Nice), as well as taxis. As in most large cities, the
area near the station is not somewhere to linger at night, though Nice-
Ville itself is safe and patrolled by uniformed security at all times.

Gare SNCF Nice-Ville ❸ av. Thiers. ❶ Information 04 92 14 82 52/53.

By bus

Long-distance and international buses arrive at Nice's *gare routière*
(central bus station), conveniently located just north of the old town
and about 10 minutes' walk to the very centre of the city, from where,
you can catch a wide variety of local buses to your onward destination.

Driving

The A8 motorway skirts the northern outskirts of Nice. If approaching
from the west turn off at junction 50 either onto the *autoroute urbain
sud*, the urban freeway, which will lead you to the north of the centre,
or follow signs to the promenade des Anglais to arrive on the seafront
itself. Make sure you adjust quickly to slow-moving traffic and watch
out for one-way systems as you approach the centre. It's a good idea to
park as soon as you approach the centre. If you take the urban freeway
turn off towards 'Gare SNCF' and park at the av. Thiers car park; there is
a tourist office at the nearby rail station. If you arrive on the
promenade, the first central car park you will see is near the Musée
Masséna, 200 yards from the city's main tourist office.

FINDING YOUR FEET

Once you've arrived, you'll find that the noise and traffic, though ever-
present, are not as bad as in many Mediterranean cities. Though the
only true pedestrian zones (*zones piétonnes*) are the Vieille Ville and the
rue de France/rue Masséna, many of the boulevards also see little
traffic. The main arteries – prom. des Anglais, av. Jean Médecin and the
roads flanking the central Paillon green space – are always busy. It's
okay to cross the street at any point if there's no traffic (but check that
you know which way it should be coming – most of Nice's roads are
one-way).

Check out the personal safety tips on pages 145–146, although you

are unlikely to feel threatened in central Nice at any time. Pickpockets
are the most likely danger you'll encounter – get into the habit of
keeping your bag or purse closed and in your view. Bring a map with
you or get one from a shop or the tourist office as soon as you can;
asking directions can be frustrating when half the people you meet are
strangers to Nice as well.

Dress comfortably, and as casually as you like. However, the locals
have a low tolerance of swimwear, and shirtless men, in the streets.
Even the bus station displays a warning against 'unsuitable attire'. Save
it for the beach or your hotel balcony. You'll notice that local girls
always throw on a lightweight wrap as soon as they leave the beach.

IF YOU GET LOST, TRY ...

Excuse me, do you speak English?
Excusez-moi, vous parlez anglais?
Ekskeweh mwah, voopahrlay ahnglay?

**Excuse me, is this the right way to the old town/the city
centre/the tourist office/ the station/the bus station?**
Excusez-moi, c'est la bonne direction pour la vieille ville/au
centre-ville/l'office de tourisme/la gare/gare routière?
*Ekskewzaymwah, seh lah bon deerekseeawng poor lah veeay veel/
oh sahngtr veel/lohfeece de tooreezm/lah gahr/gahr rootyair?*

Can you point to it on my map?
Pouvez-vous me le montrer sur la carte?
Poovehvoo mer ler mawngtreh sewr lah kart?

Arènes
de
Cimiez

CIMIEZ

Route de...

Bd. Pasteur

Av. du Maréchal Lyautey

Bd. J B Vérany

B. St-Roch

Av. des Diables Bleus

Palais des Expo
Voie Malraux

Bd. Pierre Sola

Gare Riquier

CARABACEL

RIQUIER

Auberge de
Jeunesse

Av. Gallieni

Bd. du Gal Louis Delfino

Bd. Dubouchage

Bd. Carabacel

Acropolis

R. Arson

Bd. de Riquier

Fort du
Mont Alban

Corniche André de Joly

Rd. Forestière du Mont Boron

R. Barla

Av. St-Jean Baptiste

Av. St-Sébastien

Pl. Garibaldi

R. Cassini

R. F.Guizol

Rte. du Mont Alban

Gare Routière

Bd. Carnot

MONT
BORON

s. Félix Faure

Bd. Jean Jaurès

VIEILLE
VILLE

Bd. Stalingrad

PORT

1 Albert 1er

Le Château

Quai des Etats-Unis

Quai Rauba Capeu

Bd. Franck Piatte

Parc Forestier
du Mont Boron

300   600m

Bassin du
Commerce

Fort du
Mont Boron

n g e s

ORIENTATION

The centre of Nice is defined by the west-to-east seafront (promenade des Anglais, becoming the quai des Etats-Unis further east), the north–south avenue Jean Médecin, and the wide boulevard-flanked spaces of the Paillon (Nice's river, now covered over with parks and squares in the centre) coming down from the north-east and meeting Jean Médecin at place Masséna before continuing to the promenade des Anglais as the Jardin Albert 1er. The west–east top of the walkable centre is formed by the boulevard Victor Hugo, crossing Jean Médecin to become the boulevard Dubouchage. The Italianate old town (Vieille Ville, also called Vieux Nice) is a triangular pocket of narrow streets and alleyways formed by the Paillon and the seafront, its third side being the green bulk of the Château hill. On the other side of the Château is the Port area. Between Jean Médecin, Victor Hugo and the promenade is the other main area of hotels, shops and restaurants, at its heart the pedestrian zone of rue de France and rue Masséna.

The maps in this book are up to date and show all the main sights and streets in each area, but many of the places that we list are on smaller streets. If you are planning to stay in Nice for longer than a couple of days, it's a good idea to acquire a detailed map , preferably one with a street index, from a local news-stand or bookshop or from the tourist office.

GETTING AROUND

It's no hardship to walk – the entire length and breadth of the centre is no more than a 30–40-minute walk in any direction. For sights outside this area, you'll need catch a bus or train.

Buses

Nice has an excellent bus system, day and night (night buses are called Noctambus), run by the regional company Ligne d'Azur (www.lignedazur.com). The buses are single-decker, clean, comfortable and safe. A detailed bus map, which covers the city and most of the outlying places mentioned in this book, is obtainable from the tourist offices, but not, strangely, from the central bus station. All bus stops display their names, clear maps and timetables for the routes that serve them. The company also allows you to download a timetable for each of its routes from its website, which is worth doing if you have particular destinations in mind, because the helpdesk at the central bus station is not very generous with them.

A single journey anywhere in Nice costs €1.30, payable to the driver on boarding (always board at the front). He can also sell you a one-day pass (€4 for unlimited travel by one person in one day), a 7-day pass (€15, unlimited travel by one person in 7 consecutive days) or a multi-ticket (€20, which is good for 17 person-journeys and can be used by one or more people simultaneously). *Tabacs* (tobacconist shops, which display a red diamond sign outside) sell 10-journey multi-tickets, too. Always remember to stick your ticket in the little validation machine when you first board the bus. When you want to get off, ring the bell before the stop and dismount from the door in the middle of the bus, not the front.

Nice is also busy building the second tramway line in its history (the original 1880 line gave way to trolleybuses in 1953), scheduled to open at the end of 2006. This has turned the entire length of the central av. Jean Médecin into a building site, causing buses to be rerouted and creating a maze of temporary footpaths for shoppers. When complete the tramway will provide a quick and easy way of navigating between the shops of av. Jean Médecin, the central bus station and the old town.

CIMIEZ

Musée Chagall

Voie Malraux   17

CARABACEL

15 30.

Bd. Dubouchage

Bd. Carabacel 4, 30.

10, Rue des Hôtels/Auberge hostel

Av. Galliéni

Acropolis

Palais des Expo

Bd. J.B. Vérany

Av. du Maréchal Juin

Bd. Pierre Sola

RIQUIER

Bd. du Gal Louis Delfino

R. Arson

R. 1, 2, 7, Bd. de Riquier

30   R. Barla

Av. Jean Baptiste

Av. St-Sébastien

P. Garibaldi

R. Cassini

R. F. Guizol

1, 2, 7

Giofredo

Bd. Dubouchage

1, 2, 7, 14, 81.

Gare Routière

1, 2, 7, 14, 81.   14. 81. Bd. Carnot

Port

Bd. Félix Faure   Stn Bermond

Bd. Jean Jaurès

VIEILLE
VILLE

Terra Amata
Mont Boron

Le Château

Quai des Etats-Unis

Quai Rauba Capeu

Bassin du
Commerce

0   300   600m

Trains

Local trains aren't much use to visitors for travelling within the city, but they are a great way to travel along the coast and into the mountains – see page 108.

Taxis

Not a cheap option in Nice, especially at night rates (19.00–07.00). You can pick up a cab from ranks at espace Masséna, prom. des Anglais, pl. Garibaldi (near MAMAC), rue de l'Hôtel des Postes (at the back of Galeries Lafayette) or the main rail station. Otherwise call: Central Taxi Riviera. ☎ 04 93 13 78 78. ⏱ 24 hours 7 days a week.

Driving

To drive from one sight in central Nice to another would be slower than walking, but if you are staying outside the centre and driving in every day, you won't find any shortage of covered car parks. On-street parking is hard to find, but if you do find it you can expect other drivers to park so close that you can't get away when you want to.

Car hire

If you want to hire a car, it's better and cheaper to do it in advance through your travel agent, airline or one of the main auto rental companies' central booking systems on the web. If it's a spur-of-the-moment decision, all of the major rental companies and many local ones have offices around the main rail station, **Gare Nice-Ville** ⓐ av. Thiers. (For airport car rentals, see page 51). A comprehensive list of locations is available on the tourist office website. Many hotels can arrange car hire and usually have the car brought to the hotel.

● *The Vieille Ville often looks more Italian in places than French*

THE CITY OF
Nice

Old Nice & the Port

The Château hill and the port below it was where the ancient Greeks settled to found Nikaia. Later, the medieval town grew up to the west in the triangle now known as the Vieille Ville (old town) or Vieux Nice. This is a partly pedestrianised maze of narrow streets opening out onto small squares, whose centre is the busy open space of the cours Saleya, which adjoins the seafront of quai des Etats-Unis at the old fish market buildings. Apart from one or two municipal buildings, the look and feel of its colourful architecture is pure Italy, with a dash of North African *souk* at the north-east end.

WHAT'S IN A NAME?
You will notice that, in deference to Nice's past, most of the street names in the Vieille Ville are displayed in both French and the local dialect Nissard or Nizzarda, no longer an everyday language.

SIGHTS & ATTRACTIONS

Rue St-François-de-Paule
Enter the Vieille Ville from the Jardin Albert 1er along this shop-lined street, which takes its name from the 18th-century church of St Francis of Paola (a popular French–Italian Renaissance friar, now officially the patron saint of Italian fishermen) on the left. Almost opposite is the city's Opéra, an imposing 1885 imitation of Garnier's Paris opera house.

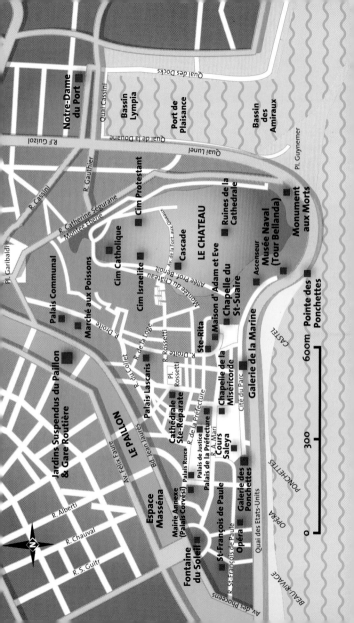

Notre-Dame du Port

Quai des Docks

Bassin Lympia

Quai Cassini

Port de Plaisance

Quai de la Douane

Bassin des Amiraux

Quai Lunel

Pl. Guynemer

R. F Guizol

R. Cassini

R. Gauthier

R. Catherine Ségurane

Montée Éberle

Pl. Garibaldi

Cim Protestant

Cim Catholique

LE CHATEAU

Ruines de la Cathédrale

Cascade

Av. de la Font. aux Oiseaux

Cim Israélite

Montée du Château

Allée Prof. Benoît

Maison d' Adam et Eve

Chapelle du St-Suaire

Ascenseur

Musée Naval (Tour Bellanda)

Monument aux Morts

Palais Communal

Marché aux Poissons

R. Droite

R. de la Loge

R. Rossetti

R. du Collet

R. Droite

R. du Collet

Palais Lascaris

Pl. Rossetti

Ste-Rita

Chapelle de la Miséricorde

Cité du Parc

Galerie de la Marine

CASTEL

Pointe des Ponchettes

PONCHETTES

600m

Jardins Suspendus du Paillon & Gare Routière

LE PAILLON

Av. Félix Faure

Bd. Jean Jaurès

Cathédrale Ste-Réparate

R. de la Préfecture

Cours Saleya

R. A. Mari

Espace Masséna

Mairie Annexe (Palais Corvesi)

Palais Rusca

Palais de Justice

Palais de la Préfecture

R. Alberti

R. Chauval

R. S. Guitr

Fontaine du Soleil

St-François de Paule

R. St-François de Paule

Opéra

Av. des Phocéens

Galerie des Ponchettes

Quai des Etats-Units

OPERA

BEAU-RIVAGE

0   300   600m

Cours Saleya

The rue St-François-de-Paule opens into this, the very heart of the old town, thronged by visitors day and night. The colourful Flower Market takes place every Tues–Sat morning, accompanied by produce and craft stalls. Every square inch is reclaimed for restaurant tables as soon as the market departs. On Monday mornings the flowers give way to *brocante*, that useful French word covering everything from genuine antiques to junk. Two churches overlook the cours Saleya: the Chapelle de la Miséricorde of 1740, with a magnificent baroque interior, and at the very end, on the corner of rue Gilly, the gold-coloured facade of the Chapelle St-Suaire, built for the use of the 17th-century judicial body, the Sénat.

Palaces

Midway along, cours Saleya opens out onto the place Gautier, whose backdrop is the white Palais de la Préfecture, formerly the Palace of the Dukes of Savoy, built in the 17th century for use by the city's Italian rulers and now the seat of the Prefect of the Alpes-Maritimes *département*. Further along the rue Alexandre Mari from the Préfecture is the neo-classical Palais de Justice (law courts), dominating the wide place du Palais, where every doorway is adorned with lawyers' brass plaques; across the square is the Palais Rusca, with its jolly pink clock tower.

Rue de la Poissonnerie

On the corner of his narrow street, heading north from the eastern end of cours Saleya, you can see the last remaining decorated house in the Vieille Ville, the Maison d'Adam et Eve, dating from the 16th

---

◑ *The narrow streets of the Vieille Ville all seem to lead to the cathedral*

RUE
SAINT-VINCENT
CARRIERA
SAN-VINCENT

century. Tucked away on the opposite side a little farther up is the 17th-century Eglise de Ste-Rita (also known as the Chapelle de l'Annonciation), dedicated to the patron saint of hopeless cases; the recently restored interior is a baroque jewel.

Cathédrale de Ste-Réparate

North of the rue de la Poissonnerie the old town becomes a warren of crowded but traffic-free alleys and streets. Follow the signs to 'Cathédrale' and you'll arrive in the place Rossetti, a lively mass of café tables surrounding an 18th-century fountain, and Nice's cathedral, dedicated to the 3rd-century Palestinian martyr Saint Reparata. The ornate plasterwork and bright colours, inside and out, are the baroque style at its most Mediterranean; Ste-Réparate was built between 1650 and 1757, replacing the original hilltop cathedral (see opposite). Don't miss the interior or the polychrome-tiled roof of the dome.

Rue Droite

One of the most direct paths through the old town, the rue Droite comes out at the place St-Francois, where you'll see the old town hall and on most mornings the lively fish market. En route it's easy to walk straight by the Palais Lascaris, a perfectly preserved aristocratic town house, which appears as little more than a doorway onto the street. Enter and discover the monumental staircase and upstairs staterooms housing art exhibitions, including material on loan from the (currently closed) Musée Masséna. Highlights are the decorated ceilings of the entrance hall, the recreated apothecary's shop just inside the door and the first-floor chapel, used for noble family weddings.

Palais Lascaris ❷ 15 rue Droite. ❶ 04 93 62 05 54. ◷ 10.00–18.00; closed Tues and some holidays. Admission free.

Le Château

This commanding hill and public park was once the centre of power of the ancient Greek city of Nikaia and of the Dukes of Savoy, and was also the site of Nice's first cathedral of Ste-Marie, the ruins of which can still be seen at the top of the hill. The Château's fortifications were strong enough to withstand a combined Franco-Turkish siege in 1543; subsequent French assaults in 1691 and again in 1705 were more successful, and in 1706 Louis XIV ordered the demolition of the castle from which the hill takes its name. From 1783 the northern side began to be used as a burial ground – Catholic, Protestant and Jewish cemeteries still occupy this area – but in 1821 the city council had the happy idea of creating a public park, which was laid out in its present form after 1860.

Today Le Château is a great place for strolling and taking in stunning views of the old town, the port and the sea. If you are the energetic type you can walk the steps leading from the end of the rue Rossetti, or take the easy way and use the *ascenseur* (lift) at the seafront end. Atop the hill are several kilometres of easy walking paths, leading you to the ruins of the medieval cathedral, an orientation table and a cooling cascade facing the Vieille Ville, as well as a café and a children's playground. Note the interesting modern mosaics in pavements and steps on the eastern side. It's an easy walk down, either back to the old town or to the port.

Château lift ❷ End of the quai des Etats-Unis, near the Hotel Suisse. 🕔 08.00–20.00 (19.00 autumn/spring, 17.30 winter). Costs €0.70 one way

The Port

Nice's port is home to some very luxurious yachts in the marina (Port du Plaisance and Bassin Lympia), from where you can also take

day-trips by boat to destinations such as Monaco, St-Tropez and the Ile Ste-Marguerite. A free shuttle bus will take you from any part of the quayside to the commercial port, which serves the giant car ferries to Corsica and Sardinia as well as the many Mediterranean cruise ships which call at Nice. The atmosphere of the Port de Plaisance is laid-back by day and night; the quaysides are where you will find some of the best bars and seafood restaurants in Nice. From here it's an easy stroll back around the foot of the Château hill along the Pointe des Ponchettes and onto the main seafront of the quai des Etats-Unis.

CULTURE

If you want a complete change from the Vieille Ville's stunning array of baroque churches, head for the seafront and check out the changing exhibitions of up-and-coming artists' work at the Galerie des Ponchettes and Galerie de la Marine. Less easy to find is the Musée Naval, housed in the old fort of Tour Bellanda, up a flight of steps from the end of the quai des Etats-Unis near the Château lift. Even if you've no special interest in ships, this small collection of paintings, weapons, navigational instruments and intricate model ships is worth the climb.

Galerie des Ponchettes ⓐ 77 quai des Etats-Unis. ☏ 04 93 62 31 24. 🕑 10.00–18.00, daily except Mon, admission free.

Galerie de la Marine ⓑ 59, quai des Etats-Unis. ☏ 04 93 62 37 11. 🕑 10.00–18.00, daily except Mon, admission free.

◐ *The east side of the Château overlooks the Port and Mont Boron*

Musée Naval ❷ Tour Bellanda, quai des Etats-Unis. 🕒 Jun–Sept,
Wed–Sun, 10.00–12.00 and 14.00–19.00 (closes at 17.00 Oct–May,
and closed throughout Nov and Dec). Admission charge.

RETAIL THERAPY

Aside from the flower and produce markets, cours Saleya has a
colourful night market of gifts, crafts, toys and the like, which range
from the desirable to the weird. On Monday mornings the *brocante*
market is worth browsing for antiques, militaria, craft items and old
cast-offs. If you see something you really like and you've got the
time, it's worth bargaining. The pl. du Palais hosts specialist markets
on Saturdays between 08.00 and 18.00: second-hand books (1st and
3rd Sats); paintings and crafts (2nd Sat); old postcards (4th Sat).

The Vieille Ville itself is packed with shops, high-quality specialist
boutiques mingling with mass-market outlets.

Au Brin de Soleil High-quality Provençal style in fabrics, kitchenware
and painted articles. ❷ 1 rue de la Boucherie. 🕒 Daily 09.30–19.30.

L'Atelier des Jouets The place to go for something special in toys,
almost too good to give to children! ❷ 1 pl. de l'Ancien Sénat.
🕒 Daily 10.30–19.00, except Wed mornings.

Poterie Painting encourages you to create a truly unique souvenir by
designing and painting your own pottery; your (or your children's)
artistic efforts are then glazed and fired ready to take away.
❷ 1 rue du Pont Vieux. ☎ 04 93 80 51 77. 🕒 Daily 10.00–19.00.

⏵ *Shops and restaurants surround the Port de Plaisance*

Quartier des Antiquaires is the place for real antique shops; in particular, the **Village Ségurane**, on the corner of rue Catherine Ségurane and rue Gauthier, is a two-storey mall of quality antique outlets. 🄰 Around rue Gauthier, on the eastern side of the Château hill.

Saint James The Nice branch of this French chain of sportswear and fashion shops is in the Port area and, appropriately, sells very nautical and *matelot*-looking striped jerseys and tee-shirts as well as other smart casual clothing. 🄰 11 pl. Ile de la Beauté. 🄱 04 92 00 01 91.

TAKING A BREAK

The choice of cafés for a quick coffee or drink or a light lunch is limitless. The liveliest areas are the cours Saleya and the place Rossetti, which has the added attraction of Fenocchio, an ice cream paradise. *Socca* (see page 30), baguettes and other take-away snacks are ubiquitous, with a definite North African/Middle Eastern bias to the fare on offer where the rue Droite meets the place St-François. There's no shortage of pizzerias in the old town for a quick lunch, but a one-course seafood meal can be surprisingly cheap at one of the seafood restaurants lining the quai de Lunel at the side of the port.

Bistrot du Port Lunch on one of the day's seafood specials, with a carafe of house rosé, and enjoy the great harbour view. 🄰 28 quai Lunel. 🄱 04 93 55 21 70. 🄲 12.00–14.15, 19.30–22.30 Mon, Thu–Sun; lunchtime only Tues; closed Wed.

▶ *Place Rossetti is a major hangout by day or night*

Fenocchio This old-established ice cream parlour offers more flavours than you would have thought possible. ⓐ pl. Rossetti. ⓛ Daily.

Chez René is the classic place for socca. Service is English pub style – order food at the bar, take your drinks to one of the outside tables and wait for the food to be served. ⓐ 2 rue Miralheti. ⓛ 09.00–23.00 daily except Mon.

Maison de la Pizza The flavours from the wood-fired oven at this tiny pizzeria are heard to beat, even by Nice standards. ⓐ 2 rue Mascoïnat. ⓛ Daily.

AFTER DARK

Restaurants

Delhi Belhi €–€€ If your night out's not complete without a curry, this excruciatingly named establishment just off cours Saleya is a good choice – though be warned, the French don't share the British taste for palate-blasting spices, and you may find the fare in Nice's Indian restaurants a little milder in flavour than you are used to. ⓐ 22 rue Barillerie. ⓣ 04 93 92 51 87. ⓛ Mon–Fri only.

Lou Pistou €–€€ The name (*pistou* is pesto, a major ingredient in Provençale cuisine) hints at the authentic regional cooking on offer at this bistro near the place du Palais. You haven't tasted real *Nissard* food till you've eaten here. ⓐ 4 rue de la Terrasse. ⓣ 04 93 62 21 82. ⓛ 19.00–23.30 Mon–Fri only.

Pizza du Cours €–€€ Cours Saleya at night seems like one vast open-air restaurant, mostly serving standard but good-quality pasta, pizza and seafood. The ambience, rather than the cuisine, is the attraction. Pizza du Cours is one of the first to fill up, though, so get there by 22.00 to get an outside table. ❷ 28 cours Saleya. ❶ 04 93 80 82 95. ❸ Daily 12.00–24.00.

Don Camillo €€ Gourmet cuisine using market-fresh produce is the hallmark of this highly rated restaurant just behind the eastern end of the quai des Etats-Unis. Service is good and prices lower than the quality justifies. Booking advised. ❷ 5 rue des Ponchettes. ❶ 04 93 85 67 95. ❸ 12.00–14.00, 19.00–22.00 Mon–Sat (closed Mon lunchtime).

Tire-Bouchon €€ As a change from Italian and *Nissard* dishes, sample the classic Lyonnais cuisine of this small restaurant just

⬤ *Nice lights up as night falls*

north of the cours Saleya (booking advisable). 🅐 19 rue de la Préfecture. 🕿 04 93 92 63 64. 🕒 19.00–10.30 daily.

L'Ane Rouge €€€ 'The Red Donkey' is a long-established Michelin-starred restaurant on the eastern quay of the port: fine dining, leaning to seafood and local specialities, at the sort of prices you would expect. Booking advisable. 🅐 7 quai des Deux Emmanuels. 🕿 04 93 89 49 63 🕒 12.00–14.00, 19.00–22.00, daily except Wed.

Entertainment

Bar des Oiseaux A Nice institution, this bar/restaurant/theatre began life as a fictional creation in comedienne Noelle Perna's radio show and she opened the real version in 1998. The live jazz and live birds (in cages) add to the atmosphere and there's a 50-seat theatre putting on Noelle's satirical revues (in broad Niçois). 🅐 Corner of rue St-Vincent and rue de l'Abbaye, near place du Palais. 🕿 04 93 80 27 33; 🌐 www.bardesoiseaux.com 🕒 12.00–14.00, 19.30–23.00.

Dizzy Club Piano bar overlooking the marina in the port area that will appeal most to a 30-plus age group. Also has live music and a dance floor. 🅐 26 quai Lunel. 🕿 04 93 26 54 79. 🕒 20.00–02.30 daily.

Ghost House Small and lively disco and bar whose DJ's jazz, house, trip-hop and more, depending on the night. 🅐 3 rue Barillerie. 🕿 04 93 92 93 37. Daily 19.30–02.30.

Opéra de Nice If your taste in entertainment leans more towards the classical, the opera season runs from October to June, with a full programme of concerts, ballets, recitals and of course, opera. 🅐 4–6 rue St-François-de-Paule. 🕿 04 92 17 40 00.

Pubs If a noisy pub atmosphere with music and possibly karaoke are what you are after, take your pick in the rue Mascoïnat: favourites are the British-style **Oxford** and Dutch-style **De Klomp**.

Wayne's Well established bar/restaurant/club and self-styled 'cultural melting pot', with disco, live bands, karaoke, quiz and theme nights. The programme is so varied it's worth checking out the website. ➋ 15 rue de la Préfecture. ➊ 04 93 13 46 99; ⓦ www.waynes.fr ⓛ Daily 12.00–01.30.

Views & walks

Take an evening stroll from pl. Garibaldi, down the rue Cassini to the port. The port itself is magical at night, and one of the music bars around the harbour is likely to tempt you in for a drink or two. Continue along the quai Lunel and around the headland of the Château hill.

War memorials are not usually much of a tourist sight, but Nice's tribute to its fallen heroes is a spectacular illuminated tricolour looking out to sea from the hillside. The views out to the Mediterranean from here are unforgettable, and as you round the Pointe des Ponchettes you see the entire Baie des Anges magically defined by the lights of the seafront.

From mid-July to September the city stages a 'promenade-spectacle', La Castellada. Actors and musicians accompany an audience on a walk of the Château hill, stopping from time to time to portray the history of Nice, from the Ancient Greeks to the present day, through drama, comedy and music. You don't need a command of French to enjoy the spectacle.

La Castellada ➋ Starts from the lift ("ascenseur") to the Château (see page 67). ➊ 04 93 84 86 11. ⓛ Daily, mid July–end Aug, 20.30 for a 21.00 start. Admission charge; bookable through the tourist office.

Western Nice

Most of the sights and activities of this district are confined to the busy area extending a half-dozen blocks west of avenue Jean Médecin and south of boulevard Victor Hugo down to the seafront. Wherever you wander in this section of Nice, don't forget to look up from time to time to enjoy the upper-storey architecture of the streets – all the wealth, frivolity and self-confidence of Nice's heyday is preserved in the wonderful facades of the villas and apartment blocks built in the late 19th century, culminating in the *belle époque* (beautiful era) years before World War I. This is the area that rivals the old town in the concentration of numbers of tourists, and the establishments that cater for them. At night, especially, the seafront acts as a magnet for locals and visitors alike, providing hours of free entertainment where the actors are also the audience. Further east and north are one or two isolated attractions which are worth a journey out from the centre, including the unmissable Russian cathedral and several world-class museums.

SIGHTS & ATTRACTIONS

Promenade des Anglais

The parasol-bedecked beaches, grand hotels and casinos of the promenade des Anglais, which takes its name from the wealthy British residents who built it for their seaside strolls in the early 19th century, typify the glamorous side of Nice. Today visitors from every country in the world stroll, rollerblade or jog along the world's most famous seaside prom, accompanied, it has to be said, by a ceaseless flow of traffic, while the wealthy patrons of hotels such as the Negresco and West End breakfast, lunch or sip cocktails on their

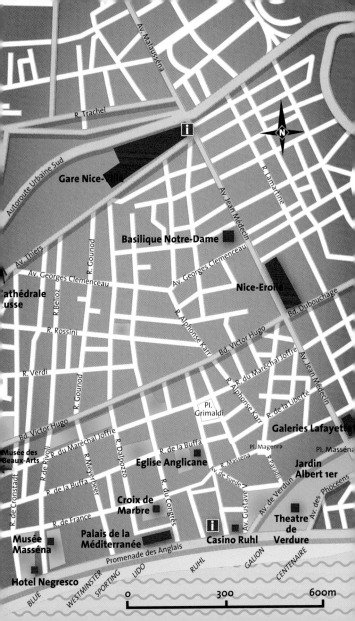

Av. Malaussèna

R. Trachel

R. Lamartine

Gare Nice-Ville

Autoroute Urbaine Sud

Av. Jean Médecin

Basilique Notre-Dame

Av. Thiers

Av. Georges Clemenceau

Av. Georges Clemenceau

Nice-Eroile

Cathédrale
usse

R. Berlioz

R. Gounod

Bd. Dubouchage

R. Rossini

R. Alphonse Karr

Bd. Victor Hugo

R. Verdi

R. Gounod

R. du Maréchal Joffre

Av. Jean Médecin

R. Alphonse Karr

R. de la Liberté

Pl.
Grimaldi

Bd. Victor Hugo

Galeries Lafayette

R. de Rivoli

R. du Maréchal Joffre

R. Meyerbeer

R. Dalpozzo

R. de la Buffa

R. Massèna

Pl. Magenra

Pl. Massèna

Musée des
Beaux-Arts

R. de Cronstadt

Eglise Anglicane

R. du Congrès

Av. de Suède

R. Paradis

Jardin
Albert 1er

R. de la Buffa

Croix de
Marbre

R. de France

Av. Gustave V

Av. de Verdun

Av. des Phocéens

Musée
Massèna

Palais de la
Méditerranée

Casino Ruhl

Theatre
de
Verdure

Hotel Negresco

Promenade des Anglais

BLUE   WESTMINSTER   SPORTING   LIDO   RUHL   GALION   CENTENAIRE

0   300   600m

glass-shielded terraces. The promenade connects with the central place Masséna via the avenue de Verdun, which along with the nearby rue de Paradis and avenue Gustave V is the favoured retail location of such upmarket icons as Cartier and Chanel. Between Verdun and avenue des Phocéens lies the park of the Jardin Albert 1er, which contains a jolly carousel for kids of all ages and the open-air Théâtre de la Verdure, scene of the free Musicalia concerts and other events.

Marking the inner part of the promenade (which carries on west for several kilometres as far as the airport) stands the pink and white wedding cake of the Hotel Negresco, *the grande dame* of Nice hotels since 1912 (see page 40). Like many old ladies, she is both stately and a little frivolous – how many hotels of her class would stand a multi-coloured plastic giant outside their front door?

The imposing building opposite the Negresco is the Villa Masséna, the former home of a descendant of Marshal Masséna (see page 15). This houses the Musée Masséna, a collection centred around the history of Nice and the early 19th century, including Napoleon's coronation robes. Unfortunately the museum has been closed for restoration for some years, though it may re-open in 2006.

Further east along the promenade is the art deco facade of the Palais de la Méditerranée. What the Negresco was to the *belle époque*, the Palais became for the Jazz Age – the hotel of choice for millionaires, presidents and the stars. Built by the Dalmas brothers for American millionaire Frank Gould in 1930, it was the wonder of the age, with a 1000-seater theatre and a casino. By 1978 it was derelict; the state declared the facade a national building, but the

● *The art deco facade hides a modern hotel*

remainder was demolished. Now a new grand hotel and casino sit, rather uncomfortably, behind Gould's masterpiece. Two blocks along Nice's other casino, the Casino Ruhl, occupies the ground floor of the Meridien hotel.

Rue de France & Rue Masséna

The side streets leading up from the promenade are a mix of designer stores, night clubs and discos, and grocery stores and fast-food outlets. Running along the top of them is the rue de France, which is pedestrianised from the junction with rue du Congrès. Nearby, facing the little place Christine Mane, is one of the few historical monuments in this part of Nice, the Croix de Marbre, a marble cross erected in 1568 to celebrate a meeting between the three most powerful men in Europe at the time, Pope Paul III, the Holy Roman Emperor Charles V and King François I of France.

Opposite the Cross, a column commemorates visits by a later pope, Pius VII. In rue de la Buffa, just north of rue de France, is a little piece of England, the Anglican Church, built for the British expatriate community in 1862. The surrounding English cemetery dates from 1820. The remainder of rue de France, leading through rue Masséna to the very centre of the city at place Masséna, is a bustling pedestrianised thoroughfare with wall-to-wall restaurants, bars and shops, thronged with visitors and street entertainers. Busy but not tacky, it has enough to keep the dedicated shopper or diner occupied for days.

Cathédrale Orthodoxe Russe St-Nicolas (Russian cathedral)

Well north of the centre of town, this has become Nice's most-visited single attraction, and remains the largest Russian Orthodox church outside the motherland. In a villa on this site in 1865 Grand Duke Nicholas, son and heir to the Russian Imperial throne, died at the age of 21. The aristocratic Russian expatriate community, led by the Czar and Czarina, had this basilica erected in his memory. It was completed in 1912, just before the Bolshevik Revolution swept away the society that built it, but was further enriched by ecclesiastical treasures that the fleeing nobility smuggled out of Russia. Today it is the mother church of Nice's new Russian community and its gilded onion domes guard a jewel box of icons and opulent frescoes. The self-guide sheets given to visitors explain the iconography in great detail and there is a nice selection of reproduction icons for sale in the vestibule. As you walk along blvd Tzarewitch to the cathedral from the bus stop, glance to your right to admire the art deco facade of the apartment block known as Le Palladium.

ⓐ blvd du Tzarewitch, north of the main rail station.

ⓛ Daily 09.00–12.00, 14.30–18.00 Jun–Sept and 14.30–17.30

● *The fairytale roofline of the Russian cathedral*

Oct–May; closed for Mass 10.00–12.00 Sun. Admission charge.
Ⓝ Buses 4 and 7: Thiers-Gambetta; then walk under the motorway bridge to cross the road and turn left into blvd Tzarewitch.

CULTURE

Musée des Beaux-Arts J. Chéret (Fine Arts Museum)

This museum stands in the western suburb of Les Baumettes. The beautiful former private villa, built in 1876, of a Russian princess houses a fine collection of paintings, from 17th-century Italian works to 19th and 20th-century Romantics and Impressionists, including Degas, Boudin, Dufy and Sisley, as well as sculptures by Rodin and others. It is particularly strong in pieces by Nice's native masters Van Loo and Chéret.

ⓐ 33 av. des Baumettes. ❶ 04 92 15 28 28. 🕐 10.00– 18.00 daily except Mon and some public holidays. Admission charge. Free to under-18s and free to all on 1st and 3rd Sun of month. Ⓝ Bus 38: Musée Chéret.

Musée des Arts Asiatiques (Oriental Art Museum) & Parc Phoenix

In complete contrast, this is a 1998 minimalist building, a work of art in its own right designed by Japanese architect Kenzo Tange to embody Asian philosophical principles. The museum is a series of individual galleries, each devoted to a different Eastern civilisation, from China and Japan to Cambodia and India. There is also a Japanese tea-room where you can experience an authentic tea ceremony and a multimedia centre for further study of Asiatic culture. The museum stands in the grounds of Parc Phoenix, 7 hectares (17 acres) of floral displays laid out on an ecological theme; the world's largest glasshouse houses the tropical plants. The park puts on a varied programme of exhibitions; for details visit Ⓦ www.nice.fr and follow links under 'Nice Métropole'. Although these two attractions are a bus journey to the edge of town, they are well worth the trip.

ⓐ 405 prom. des Anglais, close by the airport. ⓣ 04 92 29 37 00;
ⓦ www.arts-asiatiques.com ⓛ 10.00–18.00 (17.00 mid-Oct–end Apr);
closed Tues and some public holidays. Admission charge.
ⓝ Buses 9, 10 and 23: Arénas.

Musée d'Art Naïf Anatole Jakovsky (Museum of Naive Art)

Western Nice's trio of destination museums is completed by Jakovsky
Museum, opened in 1982 in the Château Sainte-Hélène, former
residence of the *parfumier* François Coty. Over 600 paintings, drawings,
engravings and sculptures chart the world of naive art from the 18th
century to the present, including works by Bauchant, Bombois, Rimbert,
Séraphine and Croatian, Haitian and Brazilian artists.

ⓐ av. de Fabron. ⓣ 04 93 71 78 3. ⓛ 10.00–18.00 daily except Tues and
some public holidays. Admission charge. ⓝ Buses 9, 10, 11, 12, 23 and 34:
Fabron-Musée d'Art Naïf.

RETAIL THERAPY

Fashion boutiques and shoe shops crowd the sides of the *zone
piétonne*. None of them stand out as destination shops, but they all
offer more individual and original items than the big stores. Check out
Un Jour en Provence, ⓐ 13 rue Masséna, if you are looking for a more
authentic alternative to the mass-produced Provençal fabrics on offer
at most other shops.

Near the eastern end of rue Masséna, leading down from the small
place Magenta, is rue Paradis, one of Nice's centres for international
designer names, including Max Mara, Armani, Chanel, Gladys Falk and
Sonia Rykiel. More famous names – Cartier, Hermes, Lacoste, Louis
Vuitton, Yves St-Laurent to name but a few – can be found round the
corner on the av. de Verdun and av. de Suede.

TAKING A BREAK

Cafés, bars, pizzerias and ice cream parlours abound in the *zone piétonne* and surrounding streets. Most open early morning and only shut when the last customer has gone home.

Caffè de la Promenade, a neon-lit Italian-style café and ice-cream parlour, is great for watching the endless procession of life along the seafront.  Corner of prom. des Anglais and rue Halévy.

La Fontaine, positioned where the rue Masséna opens out enough to admit a lot more tables, is one of the best cafés for sitting over a

● *Small boutiques cluster in the rue Masséna*

coffee or a drink and watching the world go by. ❷ place Magenta.

Mori's Bar is good for a late-morning thirst-quencher, serving an exceptional range of international beers with complimentary dishes of luscious Provençale olives. ❷ 5 rue de France.

Le Québec For a more substantial midday pit-stop, a lot of experts rate the pizzas at this busy restaurant as the best in town, and the size of the place guarantees you won't have to wait long, if at all, for a table – great atmosphere at night, too. ❷ 43 rue Masséna; ● 11.00–01.00.

La Rotonde If you are smartly dressed and want to treat yourself, why not book a lunch table at the brasserie in the Negresco – it's nothing like as expensive as the upmarket ambience might suggest, and you might spot some well known faces! (See details on pages 89–90.)

AFTER DARK

Restaurants
Every national cuisine imaginable is available around here, too many to list. If you head off the main thoroughfares into the quieter north–south cross streets you're bound to make your own discoveries and save a little off the bill.

Texas City € 'French-Texan' owner Frank Charat lays on a satisfying array of Tex-Mex food and hamburgers, with the bonus of proper cocktails. ❷ 10 rue Dalpozzo. ❶ 04 93 16 25 75. ● Daily 12.00–14.00, 19.00–23.00 (closed Sun lunchtime).

Noori's €–€€ Well reviewed Indian restaurant just off the main pedestrianised zone. Mumbai cuisine, good service. ⓐ 1 pl. Grimaldi. ⓣ 04 93 88 80 87. ⓛ Daily 19.00–23.30.

Taverne Masséna €–€€ Unashamedly catering for tourists, in one of the busiest locations of the city, the Taverne nevertheless serves up genuine and hearty brasserie food – onion soup, choucroute, seafood and other standards – in decent portions. The walls are decorated with figures from Nice's history, including inevitably Marshal Masséna. ⓐ 25 rue Masséna. ⓣ 93 87 77 57. ⓛ Daily 11.30–00.30.

Boccaccio €€ The unmissable blue art nouveau facade signals the place to go for serious seafood, served by serious bow-tied waiters. The paella is the best you'll taste in Nice. Arrive early or book ahead if you want one of the restricted number of outdoor tables; inside the decor is on a sailing ship theme. ⓐ 7 rue Masséna. ⓣ 04 93 87 71 76. ⓛ Daily 09.30–15.00, 18.00–24.00.

Karr €€ Elegant but affordable French and international cuisine, plus a stylish lounge bar with resident DJ. ⓐ 10 rue Alphonse Karr. ⓣ 04 93 82 18 31. ⓦ www.karr.fr ⓛ Mon–Sat 19.30–23.30 (bar from 18.30).

Luc Salsedo €€ Located on a quiet side street, this is a newcomer to the Nice restaurant scene, though the young chef whose name is over the door has trained with the best. Cosy pink decor and a small menu (changed every ten days) offering original variations on Mediterranean cuisine. ⓐ 14 rue Maccarani. ⓣ 04 93 82 24 12. ⓛ Daily for lunch and dinner, except Wed and Thur evening.

Maison de Marie €€ This courtyard restaurant is accessed from the busy rue Masséna just by Boccaccio (see opposite) but is a world away from the bustle of the pedestrian zone, an oasis of calm, good Provençal cooking and friendly, attentive service. Booking advisable. 🅐 5 rue Masséna. 🕿 04 93 82 15 93; 🆆 www.lamaisondemarie.com 🕓 Daily 12.00–14.00, 19.00–23.00.

La Rotonde €€–€€€ The convivial atmosphere of Bruno Turbot's brasserie in the Hotel Negresco includes an indoor fairground

● *Boccaccio is a Nice institution*

carousel, and the set menu is very reasonably priced. Booking advised. For more formal and expensive dining in opulent Regency surroundings, book for the Michelin-starred restaurant **Le Chantecler** – same location, same chef. ❸ Hotel Negresco, 37 prom. des Anglais. ❶ 04 93 16 64 00. ⏰ Daily 07.00–24.00.

ENTERTAINMENT

The area just behind the promenade is the place to hunt out late-night discos and bars with dancing, some advertising cabaret with showgirls. These streets can get a bit sleazy late at night, so don't leave a disco alone.

Smart dress and a small entrance fee (and your passport, if you intend to gamble) will get you into the two big casinos on the promenade. A casino visit can be a total night out – both have bars and restaurants that are a big attraction in themselves and put on special themed nights (Creole, Spanish, Tex-Mex evenings, and so on) in the summer season. For a separate admission charge you can watch a Las Vegas style show and dance to a disco afterwards at the Ruhl, and the Palais stages cabaret and other performance events

KNOW YOUR ROULETTE

For the uninitiated, French roulette is the kind where everybody crowds round the table, while the English version has a limited number of table seats and the players all bet in chips of their own colour (so much more orderly). American roulette gives the bank two chances of taking everyone's money, with a zero and a double zero on the wheel during the winter, and also hosts the Miss Nice contest (if you're thinking of entering, you need to be female, 18–23 and French).

Le Queenie Lively brasserie next to the Palais de la Méditerranée, catering particularly to groups. This is one place that serves the hearty Provençal fish stew *bouillabaisse* on demand at any time. Live music eight till late on Fri, Sat and Mon nights and wide-screen football – English Premiership and UEFA games. ⓐ 19 prom. des Anglais. ⓣ 04 93 88 52 50; ⓦ www.queenie.fr ⓞ Daily.

Casino Ruhl boasts 350 slot machines and 5 blackjack, 6 English and 5 French roulette and 4 poker tables. ⓐ 1 prom. des Anglais; ⓣ 04 93 87 95 97; ⓦ www.accorcasinos.com/casinos/nice.shtml

Palais de la Méditerranée has 4 blackjack, 2 stud poker, 6 American and 2 French roulette tables. ⓐ 15 prom. des Anglais. ⓣ 04 92 14 68 00; ⓦ www.partouche.com

Hitting the Promenade

Everyone in Nice hits the promenade des Anglais at night at least once a week. The local youth take to their cars and motorbikes, everybody else walks up and down. This is Nice's version of the Italian *passeggiata*, and the point is just to to see and be seen and to take in the night-time views of the light-fringed bay. In the summer you may well be able to catch a free concert at the Théâtre de la Verdure, but if not there will be plenty of home-grown talent – musicians and performers – on the seafront. The beach is as popular as during the day for impromptu picnics, volleyball games or just hanging out (but leave when the crowds start to thin out – it's not the safest place at night – and *never* be tempted to sleep out on it.)

Eastern Nice

East of avenue Jean Médecin, Nice is a collection of disparate areas and suburbs, without any specific focus except for the 'green belt' of the Paillon (Nice's river, now covered in parks and squares). Walking eastwards from here leads to the area just north of the port, which includes place Garibaldi and the Terra Amata Museum. Farther east of the centre are the hillsides of Mont Alban and Mont Boron, good for a quick escape into the fresh air. Last but not least, the northern middle-class suburb of Cimiez has a clutch of cultural attractions that easily justify the bus journey.

SIGHTS

Le Paillon

Leading east out of the place Masséna is avenue Félix Faure, the northern flank of the continuous open space marking the old course of the river Paillon. Espace Masséna is a large public square with fountains and greenery, looking across to the towers of the old town, which hosts local events and parades from time to time. Over the *gare routière*, the central bus station, is the rather grandly named terrace of the *Jardins Suspendus* or Hanging Gardens of the Paillon, which face the immense Lycée d' Etat Masséna, built in an exuberant style of decorated towers and cornices, a kind of Mediterranean Seaside Gothic.

Another hard-to-miss building is the vast grey monolith which houses MAMAC (see page 98) and the public library, and further north still are the Acropolis conference centre, with the Cinémathèque (see page 97) at its far end, and the Palais des Expositions trade fair hall.

Arènes de Cimiez
& Musée Matisse

Bd. de Cimiez

Av. des Arènes-de-Cimiez

Musée National
Message Biblique
Marc Chagall

Autoroute Urbaine Sud

Autoroute Urbaine Sud

Av. des Arènes-de-Cimiez

Cinémathèque
de Nice
Acropolis

Bd. de Cimiez

Av. Galliéni

Esplanade Kennedy

Av. de la République

Bd. Carabacel

N

Av. Notre-Dame

R. Barla

Nice Etoile

MAMAC

Terra Amata,
Mont Boron
& Mont Alban

Av. St-Jean-Baptiste

Bd. Dubouchage

Pl. Garibaldi

R. Cassini

Av. St-Sebastien

R. Pastorelli

Légion
Etrangère

Notre-Dame
du Port

Lycée d'Etat
Masséna

R. de l'Hôtel des Postes

R. Gioffredo

R. Catherine Ségurane

R. A. Gauthier

Av. Jean Médecin

Galeries
Lafayette

Av. Félix-Faure

Le Paillon

Jardins Suspendus
du Paillon & Gare
Routière

Village
Ségurane

Pl.
Masséna

Espace
Masséna

Bd. Jean Jaurès

PORT

Jardin
Albert 1er

VIEILLE
VILLE

Le Château

Quai des Etats-Unis

BEAU-RIVAGE

OPÉRA

PONCHETTES

CASTEL

0   300   600m

North & east of the Port

Across the boulevard St-Sébastien from MAMAC lies place Garibaldi, an elegant 18th-century square which was where Nice first expanded from the medieval confines of the Vieille Ville. The statue of Garibaldi, hero of Italian reunification, who was born in the city, looks on. Continuing along the rue Cassini, past the Quartier des Antiquaires (see page 72), and ignoring the many signs for the Foreign Legion recruitment office (you wonder how many destitute backpackers have signed on here for a lifetime of soldiering), you arrive at the neoclassical church of Notre-Dame du Port, whose statue of the Virgin overlooks the bustle of the Bassin Lympia. Beyond the port is the little hill of Castel des Deux Rois, with its children's amusement park and the prehistoric site of Terra Amata (see page 101).

Mont Boron

In theory if you keep walking eastwards you will reach the commanding hill of Mont Boron, Nice's biggest open space and a great place to unwind from the bustle of the city. In practice it's easier to take a bus from the city centre: if you catch no. 82 from the bus station you should get off at the Route Forestière stop on the northern slopes, from where you can walk to the massive 16th-century fortress of Mont Alban, 222 metres (721.5ft) above sea level, affording exceptional panoramic views of the Riviera and Italy. Alternatively, take bus no. 14 from place Masséna all the way to its terminus on the summit of the Parc Forestier du Mont Boron. By walking down the footpaths towards the sea from here you will eventually find yourself back on a bus route, the no. 81, which will

⏵ *The elegant Espace Masséna is a gateway to the Vieille Ville*

deposit you back at the *gare routière*. With its 142 pine-clad acres, 11 km of marked pathways and rare species of wild flowers, the forest of Mont Boron is a favourite haunt of joggers, botanists and walkers. There are magnificent views of St-Jean Cap-Ferrat to the east and the Baie des Anges to the west.

Cimiez

The quiet suburb of Cimiez, standing on what was the Roman settlement of Cemenelum, is home to a whole clutch of attractions, all next to one another. Tucked away in a quiet side-street at the southern tip of the suburb is one of Nice's mustn't-miss attractions, the Musée Nationale Biblique Marc Chagall. Further north lie the other major cultural sights, the Arènes, Museé Matisse and the Franciscan Monastery, all close together and served by the same bus stop. As you approach by bus you can't miss an enormous building with monogrammed windows; now an apartment block, this was once the

⏺ *The remains of Roman Nice at the Arènes de Cimiez*

hotel Excelsior Regina, where Queen Victoria stayed on her visits to Nice. The Musée Matisse stands in the grounds of the Arènes de Cimiez, the remains of the original 4000-seater Roman amphitheatre – a small one by Roman standards. Today the arena still provides entertainment for the citizens, most notably at the Jazz Festival. Nearby, the Musée Archéologique puts the visible remains of the Roman town in context. A short walk away is the Monastère Notre-Dame-de-Cimiez (the old Franciscan Monastery) and its associated church of Notre-Dame de l'Assomption. The monastery garden is a peaceful oasis of rose beds, next to a cemetery in which the artists Matisse and Dufy are buried. The monastery cloisters host open-air concerts in summer and the Franciscan Museum is worth a visit.

CULTURE

Eastern Nice is rich in cultural attractions; if you only visit a few of the museums and galleries listed below you will experience among the best of the city's masterpieces.

Cinemathèque

Founded in 1976 by Henri Langlois and dedicated to international film heritage, the Cinemathèque presents an ever-changing programme of classic films of the past, on themes based around the work of a director or performer. It also works to preserve classic films and hosts conferences. To view the forthcoming programme, visit the website; to see a film you need only turn up, become a subscriber for a fee of €1, and then pay a modest €2 per film.
🅰 At the north end of the Acropolis centre, 3 espl. de Kennedy.
🛈 04 92 04 06 66; 🅦 www.cinematheque-nice.com 🕒 Sept–July.
🚍 Buses 3–6: Acropole.

● *MAMAC's uncompromising architecture is hard to miss*

Musée d'Art Moderne et d'Art Contemporain – MAMAC (Modern Art Museum)

The permanent collection, dating from 1990, is dedicated to the related schools of French Nouveau Réaliste and American Pop Art, and pays particular attention to the Nice School of the last 30 years. There is a constantly changing programme of temporary exhibitions. Not only a must for all serious students of modern art, the pop art collection is fun for the casual visitor too.

ⓐ Promenade des Arts. ① 04 93 62 61 62; ⓦ www.mamac-nice.org
ⓛ Tues–Sun 10.00–18.00, except some public holidays. Admission charge; free on the 1st and 3rd Sun of the month.
ⓝ Buses 3, 5, 6, 16 or 17: Promenade des Arts.

Musée Archéologique de Nice-Cimiez (Archaeological Museum of Nice)

The museum charts the history of civilisation in Nice and the Alpes-Maritimes region (of which Nice was the Roman capital). The collection includes well preserved Roman baths dating back to the 2nd and 3rd centuries AD, as well as ceramics, glass, coins, jewellery, sculptures and tools ranging from the Bronze and Iron Ages to the Dark Ages. A small shop offers reproductions of some of the exhibits. ⓐ 160 av. des Arènes. ☎ 04 93 81 59 57. ⏰ Wed–Sun 10.00–18.00, closed on some public holidays. Admission charge; free 1st and 3rd Sun of the month. ⓝ Buses 15, 17: Arènes.

Musée National Message Biblique Marc Chagall (Chagall Museum of the Message of the Bible)

This museum is one of the cultural highlights of any stay in Nice. It was opened in 1972 through the efforts of Chagall himself, to house his enormous body of work on Biblical themes, consisting of paintings, sculptures, stained glass windows, mosaics and tapestries, preparatory sketches, gouaches, engravings and lithographs. The 17 large canvases that are the highlight of the exhibition were painted between 1954 and 1967; Chagall's interpretations of the *Creation of Man* and *The Garden of Eden* are particularly stunning. There are also temporary exhibits of other themes to which he returned again and again, such as the circus. The building itself is the work of André Hermant, a follower of Le Corbusier, and stands in a small garden. The on-site shop sells books and excellent reproductions of Chagall's works. ⓐ av. du Dr Ménard, corner of blvd de Cimiez. ☎ 04 93 53 87 20; ⓦ www.musee-chagall.fr ⏰ Wed–Mon 10.00–18.00 July–Sept, closes 17.00 Oct–June. Admission charge. ⓝ Bus 15: Musée Chagall.

MARC CHAGALL

Born 1887 into a poor Orthodox Jewish family in Vitebsk, now in Belarus, Chagall spent his early career in St Petersburg and Paris, where he mixed with the Fauvists, Surrealists, Cubists and other avant-garde artists of the day. After a brief spell as an official artist in Bolshevik Russia, he wandered between Berlin, New York and Paris, developing a unique style in which brilliant colour and the frequent reappearance of a range of iconic characters are the most obvious elements. In 1949 he settled in the Nice area, as had Matisse and Picasso, and died in St-Paul-de-Vence at the age of 97. He mastered an astonishing range of media, from stained glass to lithography. A deeply religious man all his life, he was inspired by a visit to the Holy Land in 1930 to begin his Biblical masterpieces.

Musée Franciscain (Franciscan Museum)

Part of the Franciscan Monastery of Cimiez, this museum is devoted to St Francis of Assisi and the history of the order which he founded, through paintings, sculptures, engravings, illuminated manuscripts, frescoes, and a reconstructed chapel and monk's cell. ❸ pl. du Monastère. ❶ 04 93 81 00 04. ❸ Mon–Sat 10.00–12.00, 15.00–18.00 except public holidays. Admission free. ❷ Bus 17: Monastère.

Musée Matisse

Housed in and underneath a handsome red-painted 17th-century villa next to the Arènes de Cimiez, the original collection was donated by the artist himself in 1953. In addition to his paintings, drawings, engravings and sculptures, many of his favourite possessions are on display. Henri Matisse, who along with Dufy is the best-known artist of the Fauve school, lived in Nice from 1917 until his death in 1954. The works on show range from his earliest paintings of 1890 to his famous gouache cut-outs, and the museum holds a copy of every book he illustrated. There is also a well stocked shop for prints and other souvenirs of Matisse and other French artists.

ⓐ 164 av. des Arènes de Cimiez. ❶ 04 93 81 08 08; Ⓦ www.musee-matisse-nice.org. 🕒 Wed–Mon 10.00–18.00, closed on some public holidays. Admission charge; free on 1st and 3rd Sun of the month. Ⓝ Buses 15, 17: Arènes.

Musée de Paléontologie Humaine de Terra Amata (Museum of Human Prehistory)

Taking its name from the earliest inhabited site to be excavated here, this well arranged museum is devoted to the 7 million-year history of Man, and specifically the last 900 millennia. The area around Nice is one of the longest-inhabited sites in Europe and rich in the remains of prehistoric man. The story that Terra Amata tells is fascinating anyway, but the local finds add a special relevance; it's not everywhere that possesses a 400,000-year-old camp of elephant-hunting *Homo erectus*, who predated *Homo sapiens* by over 350,000 years and seems to have developed communication skills. Ever-changing temporary exhibitions add to the experience and the museum shop is a good place for unusual souvenirs.

ⓐ 25 blvd Carnot. ❶ 04 93 55 59 93. Ⓦ www.musee-terra-amata.org. 🕒 Tues–Sun 10.00–18.00 (closed on some holidays). Admission charge; free on 1st and 3rd Sun of the month. Ⓝ Bus 81: Gustavin (nearest stop). Buses 1, 2, 9 and 10: Port Arson, a walk of about 200 metres from the museum.

RETAIL THERAPY

The east side of avenue Jean Médecin is dominated by the Galeries Lafayette department store on the corner of place Masséna and a two blocks north there's a day's worth of shopping at the multi-storey Etoile centre, with over 200 shops and specialist boutiques, including familiar names such as Habitat, and a branch of FNAC: this chain sells books (including English-language), CDs and electronic and photographic products, and is the place to buy tickets for concerts and other events. The avenue is also a centre for bags and leather goods, with at least ten specialist shops. Shops on the streets east of Jean Médecin tend to be for local, practical needs, but include some specialists.

ArtDecoRoom If you're a fan of art deco and other styles of the 1920s and 30s, then this place sells beautiful authentic objects of the period – at a price. They also have a branch in the Quartier des Antiquaires (see page 72). ❸ 5 rue Gioffredo; ❶ 04 93 92 91 69; Ⓦ www.artdecoroom.com

Bruno Charvin Arts has everything a budding Renoir or Matisse could desire; you might not be able to get one of their massive easels onto the plane but there are plenty of other smaller artists' items which make good presents from the City of Art. ❸ 39 rue Gioffredo; ❶ 04 93 92 99 90.

The Cat's Whiskers The place to go if you've forgotten to bring holiday reading, specialising in English-language books. ❸ 30 rue Lamartine; ❶ 04 93 80 02 66.

---

❶ *If you're an artist rather than an art collector, head for Bruno Charvin*

La Maison Provençale While you're in the rue Gioffredo, check out this store for traditional Provençal crafts. ⓐ 18 rue Gioffredo.

TAKING A BREAK

The air-conditioned coolness of the Etoile centre has a lot to recommend it for a coffee-break during shopping; there are two cafés in the atrium and more on each shopping floor. For more traditional outdoor cafés and bars, make for the boulevard Jean Jaurès on the south side of the Paillon green space. If you're visiting the Terra Amata museum, the nearest cafés and lunch stops are in the Port area, where you'll be spoilt for choice. There is a small café in the garden of the Chagall Museum, but nothing around the Arènes area. If you are planning a day out on Mont Boron take a picnic lunch.

AFTER DARK

Restaurants

Cantine de Lulu €–€€ Home cooking in a simple bistro atmosphere from Lucien Brych, whose cuisine is drawn from the two halves of his origins, Niçois and Czech. ⓐ 26 rue Alberti. ⓣ 04 93 62 15 33. ⓛ Mon for lunch only, Tue–Fri lunch and dinner; closed Aug and New Year.

Baie d'Amalfi €€ Satisfying and authentic Italian food and wine in an elegant arcaded dining room decorated with views of the Neapolitan coast. Close to av. Jean Médecin. ⓐ 9 rue Gustave Deloye. ⓣ 04 93 80 01 21; ⓦ www.baie-amalfi.com ⓛ Daily except Sun evening and all day Mon, and closed all July.

Brasserie Flo €€ A stone's throw from pl. Masséna, this brasserie, part of the same group that owns the legendary Bofinger and Boeuf sur le Toit in Paris, is a destination in its own right. Taking its cue from the original use of its building by the Folies-Bergères, Flo is set out as a theatre; the diners are the audience and the kitchen is actually on stage. The dishes are imaginative and very reasonably priced; there is even a special menu for late-night diners.
ⓐ 4 rue Sacha Guitry. ⓣ 04 93 13 38 38; ⓦ www.flonice.com
ⓛ Daily 12.00–14.30, 19.00–24.00.

Grand Café de Turin €€ Not far from the edge of the Vieille Ville on a corner of one of Nice's liveliest squares, this seafood specialist has been famous for its *fruits de mer* for nearly 100 years. The decor is plain, the service a bit patchy at busy times, but you're unlikely to taste better shellfish in Nice. ⓐ 5 pl. Garibaldi. ⓣ 04 93 62 29 52; ⓦ www.cafedeturin.com ⓛ Daily 08.00–23.00.

L'Horloge €€ Part of the revamped Grand Hôtel Aston. One of the outside tables is the perfect place to unwind in early evening, after the traffic of the avenue has died down. Attentive service and a wide-ranging menu on a Mediterranean theme, to which one of the excellent Provençal rosés is the perfect accompaniment.
ⓐ 12 av. Félix Faure. ⓣ 04 92 17 53 09; ⓦ www.hotel-aston.com
ⓛ Daily.

L'Univers de Christian Plumail €€ Original and stylish cuisine from master chef Christian Plumail, at very affordable prices, especially if you order from the set menu, which is changed weekly. For €80 you can accompany the chef on a Saturday morning tour of the markets and then of his kitchen, followed by a private lunch. ⓐ 54 blvd Jean

Jaurès. ☎ 04 93 62 32 22; ⓦ www.christian-plumail.com
🕐 Tues–Fri for lunch and Mon–Sat for dinner.

Entertainment

Eastern Nice is not noted for a lively nightlife, but Cimiez hosts
some important annual entertainments, including:

Nice Jazz Festival First staged in 1948 (and so pre-dating the famous
Newport Jazz Festival by six years), this international celebration of
the French love affair with jazz features simultaneous performances
on several stages, alongside stalls selling instruments, discs and
books and local food and drink specialities. Over 500 musicians
participate in 120 separate performances. The festival spills over into
the town as artists make for clubs, bars and hotels to continue after
their official sessions. Even if your interest in jazz is minimal, the
atmosphere of this family-friendly event (with its own 'children's
village' for 5–12 year-olds run by qualified supervisors) makes for a
great evening. ❸ Arènes de Cimiez. ☎ (ticket sales): 08 92 70 75 07;
ⓦ www.nicejazzfest.com 🕐 Late July, 19.00–24.00.

Les Nuits Musicales de Nice, a festival of chamber music, follows on
from the Jazz Festival at the end of July and extends into early
August. Two weeks of night-time open-air performances in the
cloisters of the Franciscan Monastery in Cimiez.
☎ (ticket sales) FNAC, 08 92 68 36 22;
ⓦ www.hexagone.net/music/nuits_musi_prog.htm.
🕐 Late July–early Aug.

▶ *St-Paul-de-Vence preserves its medieval atmosphere*

Seeing the Riviera

One of the great things about Nice is that it's so easy to leave it. Not that you are necessarily going to tire of the city quickly, but it is the best possible centre for visiting other parts of the Riviera, the mountainous backdrop of the Alpes-Maritimes and even Italy. The excursions in the following chapters are only a few of the days out that are possible using Nice's excellent transport connections.

TRIPS BY TRAIN

The excellent coastal rail service from the main rail station, Gare Nice-Ville (see page 51) puts you in close touch with the rest of the coast, with literally dozens of trains per day. The train is a cheap, comfortable and quick way to visit these evocative Côte d'Azur destinations. Buy tickets at the machines found at all rail stations on this route; they are easy to use, have instructions in English and give change.

Heading east: Villefranche-sur-Mer (12 mins); Beaulieu-sur-Mer (15 mins); Monaco (25 mins); Roquebrune (30 mins); Menton (37 mins) and Ventimiglia (52 mins).

Heading west: Cagnes-sur-Mer (17 mins); Antibes (29 mins); Juan-les-Pins (32 mins); Cannes (40 mins) and Grasse (1 hr 9 mins).

Chemins de fer de Provence The trains of this private rail company depart from their own station, a couple of blocks north of Nice-Ville. You'll need to catch a no. 18 bus from the centre of town to reach the station. Their historic Train des Pignes, the 'Pine-Cone Line' (no

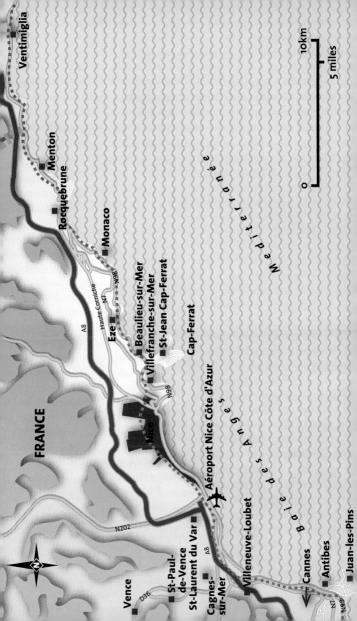

one knows for sure where the name comes from) follows the route of the river Var up into the mountains and then swings west to Digne-les-Bains, with plenty of stops in between for those who want to see a mountain village or two and do some walking. The full scenic route takes just over 3 hours, with two daily trains in each direction. Digne-les-Bains is a quaint, medieval spa town; it's still possible to take the naturally hot waters, which are said to be good for rheumatism. Until 2005 it was possible to take a special trip along the section of the line on a 1909-era stream train; this service may be resumed in 2006 – check the website under 'Train à Vapeur'.

ⓐ 4 bis rue Alfred Binet. ☏ 04 97 03 80 80.

ⓦ www.trainprovence.com

ⓝ Bus 18: Chemins de Fer de Provence.

▶ *Cap Ferrat has some of the best beaches on the Riviera*

TRIPS BY BUS

Buses depart from Nice's *gare routière* or central bus station at the far end of boulevard Jean Jaurès. Services are run by Ligne d'Azur (www.lignedazur.com), the bus corporation for the Nice metropolitan area, and the regional TAM (Transport Alpes-Maritimes, www.cgo6.fr/tam-html). Timetables and fares for individual routes are easily found on the Ligne d'Azur site, less easily on the TAM site. The central bus station is divided into *quais* (platforms) and each service always runs from the same *quai*, at which the service numbers and timetables are posted.

Buses will take you to all the places served by the trains, and some which the train doesn't reach. The cost is usually about the same as the train; buses are slower, but the ride is generally more scenic and the vehicles are air-conditioned and comfortable.

Villefranche, Cap Ferrat & Beaulieu

You may not want to do all three of these destinations in one day, but it is perfectly possible. They all lie very close to the city, just east of the promontory of Mont Boron. Villefranche is pretty and historic; St-Jean Cap-Ferrat is exclusive and upmarket, but also has a zoo and good public beaches; Beaulieu is quieter, catering mainly to an older class of visitor. This excursion also takes in two great attractions, the Villas Kérylos and Ephrussi.

The SNCF train from Nice-Ville station serves Villefranche and Beaulieu; up to 20 departures and returns a day, 12 and 15 minutes journey respectively. The TAM buses no. 100 and 111 and Ligne d'Azur bus no. 81, all from Nice central bus station, are an alternative and offer better views (100 does not visit Cap Ferrat).

SIGHTS

Villefranche-sur-Mer

This laid-back and friendly small resort is perfect for families, with a picturesque harbour and a safe, sandy beach. Apart from the beach, although there are one or two cultural sights, it's the small town clinging to the slopes by the harbour that is itself the main attraction. The colourful, pastel-washed houses of this fishing port define a warren of narrow, hilly streets and alleyways, with plenty of cafés and restaurants for the thirsty and hungry visitor. One street, the covered alley known as rue Obscure, has been dated back to the 13th century.

Office de Tourisme ⓐ Jardin Binon. ⓘ 04 93 01 73 68;

● *Take in the buzz of the quayside at Villefranche*

Ⓦ www.villefranche-sur-mer.com Ⓛ Daily 09.00–19.00 Jul–Aug; Mon–Sat 09.00–12.00, 14.00–18.00 Sept–Jun.

The Citadel The port was defended by the enormous Citadel, built by the Duke of Savoy in 1557. Villefranche's deep-water outer harbour or *rade* has been strategically important for centuries; the Duke's galleys were stationed here and their commandant resided in the Palais de Marine on quai Ponchardier. Villefranche remained an important naval base for the French and latterly the US Sixth Fleet until the 1960s, and consequently used to be a rather raunchier place than it is now. Today the Citadel houses several historical and art museums, an open-air theatre and the town hall. There is an entertaining changing of the guard ceremony outside the Citadel every evening at 19.00 (July–Aug), at which two Savoyard pikemen in 16th-century uniform are relieved by the French army's Chasseurs Alpins, symbolising the dual military heritage of the fort.

Chapelle de St-Pierre (St Peter's Chapel) The quayside possesses a star attraction in this 14th-century fishermen's chapel. The attractive exterior is covered in *trompe-l'oeuil* plasterwork, but it's the interior that draws the visitors, because it was decorated in 1957 by Jean Cocteau with frescoes depicting the life and works of St Peter; the result is an artistic tour-de-force.
ⓐ quai Admiral Courbet. Ⓛ Tues–Sun 10.00–12.00, 15.00–19.00 (17.00 Oct–May). Admission charge.

St-Jean Cap-Ferrat
Cap Ferrat's green peninsula has been famous for its millionaires' villas since European society started to buy up the real estate in the 19th century, but you won't see much of them beyond their high

security gates. If you arrive by buses TAM 11 or Ligne d'Azur 81 from Nice you can enjoy a panoramic circuit of the cape, but the more active will find that the 14 km/9 mile coastal path is a walker's paradise. The port of St-Jean, once a fishing village and now a harbour full of upmarket yachts, is a pleasant place for a drink or lunch. **Zoo-Parc Cap-Ferrat** is home to 300 animals and birds, including bears, tigers, monkeys and zebras, and will please younger holidaymakers. The buses stop at St-Jean and the Zoo. There are plenty of minor delights for walkers to discover, including the **Chapelle St-Hospice** and the **lighthouse** at the southern tip of the cape. ⏱ Daily 09.30–19.00 summer, 09.30– 17.30 winter. Admission charge.

Tourist information office has its own bus stop and is a good starting point, midway between St-Jean and the Zoo ⓐ 59 av. Denis Semeria. ⓘ 04 93 76 08 90; Ⓦ www.ville-saint-jean-cap-ferrat.fr Ⓝ TAM bus 100 and Ligne d'Azur bus 81 (which stop at all the sights on the Cap): Office du Tourisme.

Villa Ephrussi de Rothschild

More correctly called the Villa Ile de France, this is a beautiful pink-and-white confection built at the beginning of the 20th century and set in immaculate gardens. Béatrice Ephrussi de Rothschild was born into a wealthy banking family and spent much of her fortune collecting works of art and antiques to fill the villa she had built. On her death in 1934 the villa was bequeathed to the Institut de France, who now own it. Her real enthusiasm was for the 18th century, which is reflected especially in the priceless porcelain collection. For once, the cliché 'treasure-house' is fully justified; you don't have to be an antiques or art enthusiast to be overwhelmed.

ⓘ 04 93 01 33 09; Ⓦ www.villa-ephrussi.com ⏱ Daily 10.00–18.00

Feb–Oct (to 19.00 Jul–Aug); 14.00–18.00 weekdays, 10.00–18.00 weekends Nov–Jan; admission charge. Ⓝ Buses as for Cap-Ferrat. Nearest stops Passable or Office de Tourisme.

Beaulieu-sur-Mer

The name means 'beautiful place' and the attractions of the site were apparent to the ancient Greek mariners who founded the town. At the end of the 19th century American millionaire and newspaper proprietor Gordon Bennett discovered this tiny fishing village and developed it into a resort for wealthy *belle époque* visitors, including Edward, Prince of Wales and Gustave Eiffel. Much of the elegant architecture dates from this time, and the town still retains a genteel air. It's the ambience rather than individual sights that attracts visitors, but there are plenty of photogenic buildings, including the Casino and the Chapelle Sancta Maria de Olivo.
Tourist office ⓐ pl. Clémenceau. ❶ 04 01 02 21; Ⓦ www.ot-beaulieu-sur-mer.fr

Villa Kérylos

Just outside Beaulieu, on the tip of a small promontory jutting into the Baie des Fourmis, stands the 'sister' of the Villa Ephrussi, the Villa Kérylos, also owned by the Institut de France and also the life's work of one obsessive individual. The archaeologist Theodore Reinach was the scion of another wealthy banking family prominent in late 19th-century France. He was inspired to re-create his vision of a patrician Greek palace that stood on the island of Delos in the 2nd century BC, and entrusted the building of his dream villa to an architect who shared his love of archaeology, Emmanuel Pontremoli. The Villa,

● *The gardens of Villa Ephrussi are an attraction in their own right*

whose name is Greek for 'kingfisher', took six years to construct, following as closely as possible the layout of the remains uncovered on Delos. It was always intended as a house to live in (in fact the founder's family continued to live here long after his death in 1928), and the interior, though faithful to the appearance of a classical Greek villa, incorporated all the modern conveniences of the time, cleverly disguised. Today it is a tour de force that delights thousands of visitors.

 04 93 01 01 44; www.villa-kerylos.com Daily 10.00–18.00 Feb–Oct (to 19.00 Jul–Aug); 14.00–18.00 weekdays, 10,00–18.00 weekends Nov–Jan. Admission charge. TAM 100, 101 and Ligne d'Azur 81: Kérylos.

CULTURE & ENTERTAINMENT

The **Les Azuriales** opera festival, held at the Villa Ephrussi de Rothschild in the first two weeks of August, has been a major event since 1997 (www.azuriales-opera.com). Beaulieu hosts a very full programme of concerts and other performances during the summer months – up-to-date details from the tourist office and its website. A regular favourite are the **Nuits Guitares** or guitar nights in the Jardin de l'Olivaie. If you have caught the roulette bug in Nice, Beaulieu has its own historic and upmarket Casino.

RETAIL THERAPY

Villefranche

Brocante market Weekly market devoted to second-hand items of all kinds and qualities. pl. Amélie Pollonais and Jardin Binon. Sun, all day.

Savonnerie de Villefranche Locally handmade soaps and scented items. **ⓐ** 10 av. Sadi Carnot. **ⓣ** 04 93 76 66 75.

Provençal market The colourful weekly produce and craft market is a good place to buy Provençal fabrics, local olives and olive oil, clothes and flowers. **ⓐ** Jardin Binon. **ⓛ** Sat 08.00-13.00.

Beaulieu

Beaulieu avoids 'designer' labels and prefers individual small boutiques, well worth checking out for classic rather than youth-oriented fashions.

TAKING A BREAK

Cafés and ice-cream parlours can be found in nearly every street of the old town of Villefranche, and near the marinas of Beaulieu and St-Jean. The comfortable terrace of Beluga in Villefranche (see page 122) is a particularly good place to sit over a cool drink watching the yachts in the harbour, and if you're serious about boats they keep a rack full of magazines on the subject.

BEACHES

If you like sand with your sea, these resorts will satisfy your requirements better than Nice itself. The beach at Villefranche is long and safe for family swimming. Aside from walking and enjoying the lush scenery, Cap-Ferrat also offers some very nice public beaches. Passable Plage is a short walk from the tourist office along the chemin de Passable; Paloma Plage is about 1 km/$^{1}/_{2}$ mile south from the port of St-Jean, heading towards the Pointe St-Hospice, and there is another beach just north of the port. Beaulieu has two very pleasant beaches, the Baie des Fourmis (*fourmis* means 'ants', but don't worry, it refers to the little black rocks that dot the area) and the Petite Afrique.

ACTIVITIES

The excellent beach provides all the activity many visitors need, but if you prefer to get closer to the Med there are plenty of opportunities at Villefranche for boat trips, whale-watching and diving.

Affretement Maritime Villefranchois run boat trips of 1–2 hours around Cap Ferrat and as far as Monaco and Menton and back (without stopping); they also offer a 4-hour 'Mediterranean photo safari' to see dolphins and rorqual and cachalot whales. ⓐ Quayside near pl. Wilson ⓣ 04 93 76 65 65. ⓛ July–Aug: Wed 08.30, Wed–Fri and Sun 13.30; June and Sept: Wed and Sun, 13.30. Booking essential.

Dark Pelican have a range of motor boats for hire by the afternoon or day. You'll need your passport as proof of identity and will have to leave a hefty deposit in cash or by cheque (not credit card), however. ⓐ 1 quai Courbet. ⓣ 04 93 01 76 54.

Centre de Plongée offer exploration diving, photo diving for children and equipment rental as well as introductions for beginners. ⓐ 16 rue du Poilu. ⓣ 04 93 01 71 04. ⓛ Departures daily, summer 10.00 and 15.00, winter 10.00 and 14.00.

▶ *No shortage of dive boats at Villefranche*

RESTAURANTS

Villefranche

Chez Hien € Seated and take-away catering in an exotic variety of styles – Indian and Oriental, Greek and Creole –in the old town just one block behind the waterfront. ❸ 4 rue du Poilu. ❶ 04 93 01 11 32. ❷ Daily 08.00–02.00.

Le Cosmo €–€€ Halfway between the quayside and the citadel, this bar and brasserie is equally convenient for lunch after the Saturday market or a late supper or drink. Excellent salads and seafood. ❸ 11 pl. Amélie Pollonais. ❶ 04 93 01 84 05. ❷ Daily 07.00–02.30.

Beluga €€ Excellent tapas and a good range of other dishes at this new restaurant and lounge bar overlooking the seafront. ❸ 3 quai Ponchardier. ❶ 04 93 80 28 34. ❷ Daily, lunch and dinner.

L'Oursin Bleu €€ The central quayside location guarantees the freshest of fish and the adventurous cuisine makes a welcome change from standard seafood dishes. ❸ 11 quai Amiral Courbet. ❶ 04 93 01 90 12. ❷ Wed–Mon, lunch and dinner.

Beaulieu

African Queen €€ Solid brasserie and pizzeria fare, but reckoned to be a cut above average in quality and the service is fast. ❸ Port de Plaisance. ❶ 04 93 01 10 85. ❷ Daily.

Le Petit Darkoum €€ First-class Moroccan cuisine with a French accent. ❸ 18 blvd Général Leclerc. ❶ 04 93 01 48 59. ❷ Dinner only, Tues–Sun, summer; Lunch and dinner, Wed–Sun, winter.

Le Métropole €€–€€€ High-class Provençal food at one of Beaulieu's long-established hotels, served with formality and efficiency in a stylish garden-terrace setting overlooking the sea. If you opt for the set menu the price is very reasonable for the quality. ⓐ 15 blvd Général Leclerc. ⓣ 04 93 01 00 08. ⓛ For lunch and dinner. Closed late Oct–late Dec.

ACCOMMODATION IN VILLEFRANCHE

Given the short journey time and frequency of the trains, staying in Villefranche and visiting Nice by day is a viable option, especially if you are travelling as a family and want to spend plenty of time on the town's sandy beach. Most options are on or near the main highway, the Moyenne Corniche, about 10–15 minutes' walk from the town centre.

Fiancée du Pirate €–€€ This splendidly named representative of the reliable Logis de France association has good-value rooms for families of four. ⓐ 8 blvd de la Corne d'Or. ⓣ 04 93 76 67 40; ⓦ www.fianceedupirate.com

La Flore €€ is another Logis member, in a renovated 19th-century building with excellent views onto the harbour of Villefranche and a good restaurant. ⓐ 5 blvd Princesse Grace de Monaco. ⓣ 04 93 76 30 30; ⓦ www.hotel-la-flore.fr

Welcome €€ This venerable establishment is the only central hotel, close to the chapel of St-Pierre and once a favourite watering-place of Jean Cocteau (who liked to mix with the sailors who frequented it in the 1920s – it's a lot more respectable now). ⓐ 3 quai Amiral Courbet. ⓣ 04 93 76 27 62; ⓦ www.welcomehotel.fr

Eze

Eze is well worth a half-day trip from Nice; it is the archetypal *village perché*, an ancient and pretty township sitting 429 m/1300 ft above sea level, with near-perfect views out to the Mediterranean. More than half a day would be spreading its charms too thinly, unless you plan to use the remainder of your time soaking up the sun in Eze-sur-Mer, the neighbouring seaside village at the foot of the precipice. However, to get from one to the other involves waiting for a bus or a long walk down (only fitness fanatics would do the two places in reverse order). The footpath is clearly signposted and is named after Nietzsche, the German philosopher who used to climb it in the 1880s. It is steep in parts and the steps, where there are any, are quite deep. The advertised time for the descent is 45 minutes – allow an hour on a hot summer's day.

As at many Mediterranean coastal sites, the population of Eze has moved periodically from coast to hill and back again according to the safety of the times. The Celts inhabited the hilltop village 2000 years ago. The Romans, living in a more secure age, founded the port of Avisio on the coast; then the Dark Ages brought raids from Moorish pirates, driving the inhabitants to re-fortify the hill – the walls and gates of Eze date from the 14th century. In the 1880s Eze was 'discovered' by Friedrich Nietzsche and from the 1920s to the 1950s was the home of Prince William of Sweden, whose villa is now a luxury hotel. In more recent times Eze has seen an influx of celebrity visitors, ranging from President Clinton and Walt Disney (a frequent guest of the Hotel Chèvre d'Or) to Tina Turner and Naomi Campbell.

GETTING THERE

The best way to see the two sides of Eze in one day is by bus to Eze Village, then by bus (or on foot down the path) to Eze-sur-Mer, with a final short ride by train from Eze-sur-Mer back to Nice. From the *gare routière* in Nice, take either the Ligne d'Azur bus 82 or TAM 112 – both leave from quai 4. There is a bus approximately every 90 minutes on most days, starting around 7.20, and the journey to Eze Village takes about 20 minutes, depending on traffic. The route takes the Moyenne Corniche – be sure to sit on the right-hand side of the bus for the best views on the outward journey. The final approach to the village is over an impressive early 20th-century viaduct, called locally the Devil's Bridge (somehow it has acquired a much older legend of a bridge-builder who narrowly avoided selling his soul to the Devil).

The SNCF coastal train stops at Eze-sur-Mer, taking a mere 15 minutes, but with no views. Ligne d'Azur bus 83 connects Eze Village with Eze-sur-Mer: there are just 7 buses a day with long waits in between – check the timetables to plan your departure as soon as you arrive at Eze Village – and the service only runs in May–September. Journey time is about 25 minutes.

Tourist office

ⓐ pl. du Général de Gaulle, near the bus stop.

ⓘ 04 93 41 26 00.

ⓦ www.eze-riviera.com; www.tourisme.fr/office-de-tourisme/eze.htm

ⓛ Daily Apr–Oct 09.00–19.00; weekdays Nov–Mar 09.00–18.30.

SIGHTS

It's a short walk up into the old town, the original fortified village once topped by a castle that was destroyed in Louis XIV's time, through the medieval Postern Gate. The unforced charm of the narrow pedestrian-only streets, and the views out to sea and across to the Alpes Maritimes, are hard to beat. As has often been remarked, it would be difficult to take a bad photograph in Eze, unless it was spoilt by other tourists getting in the picture. You have to accept that many other people have been attracted by the same sights as you, and the alleys can get a little crowded (so plan to arrive as early as the buses will let you). Unfortunately for today's tourists, the 14th-century builders of the stronghold planned the narrow streets deliberately to slow down the advance of invaders.

The oldest building in Eze is the Chapelle de Saint-Croix (also known as the Chapel of the White Penitents) of 1306. The medieval mansions of Eze's wealthier residents have now become luxury hotels, including the Chèvre d'Or and the Château Eza (see page 130). The church of Our Lady of the Assumption was designed by the Italian architect Antonio Spinelli between 1764 and 1778 to replace an old one which fell in ruins. The exterior is relatively plain, but inside Spinelli let loose with a riot of *trompe-l'oeuil*, real windows on one side being matched by fake ones on the other, a false pulpit paired with a real one, and so on; baroque at its most theatrical.

At the very summit of Eze is the **Jardin Exotique**, begun in 1949 by the then mayor on the site of the old castle. Its collection of cacti and other dry-climate plants is complemented by female statuary by Jean-Philippe Richard, placed in strategic locations to enhance (or detract from, depending on your taste) the stunning views over Cap-Ferrat and the Italian coast. An orientation table lets you work out whether it is really possible to see Corsica, as is claimed. Whether or not you like succulents or statues, the panoramas are worth the admission fee.

ⓐ rue du Château. ⓛ Daily; admission charge.

The seaside part of the town, Eze-sur-Mer (also known as Eze Bord-de-Mer), has some good beaches, mostly supervised by lifeguards, and a few cafés and restaurants, as well as the rail station on the main Nice–Ventimiglia line.

PULLING POWER

Until it became fashionable after World War II Eze was still an agricultural commune and the only feasible means of transport along its steep narrow lanes was the donkey. Two of the Provençal breed of donkeys, Nani and Nina, until recently took luggage up to the Hotel Château Eza and can be admired in their retirement stable outside the walls.

RETAIL THERAPY

The old citadel streets are filled with shops selling antiques, craft items and art, both originals and prints. Prices are as you would expect in a place visited by so many tourists, but much of the merchandise is of a better quality than the average tourist trap. In the more modern part of the village there two very popular outlets:

Fragonard The famous fragrance company has a large factory-laboratory just off the main road, at which you can take a multi-lingual

guided tour of the science and craft of perfume-making before visiting the boutique, selling a wide range of antique jewellery, embroidered household linen, traditional quilted Provençal *boutis*, glassware and wickerwork, preserves, perfumes, natural aromatic oils and other products. ➋ Moyenne Corniche. ☎ 04 93 41 05 05.
🌐 www.fragonard.com 🕐 Factory: daily 08.30–18.30 (closed 12.00–14.00 Nov–Jan). Boutique: daily 10.00–19.00 (closed 12.30–14.00 Nov–Feb).

Valery Klein This shop (a branch of a company based in the northern French crystal centre of Baccarat) does a nice line in crystalware gifts, ranging from wine glasses to chess sets to jewellery and objets d'art. ➋ pl. Général de Gaulle. ☎ 04 93 64 90 65.

TAKING A BREAK

Most cafés and lunch stops congregate in the pl. de Collette, at the foot of the old town, near the bus stop. All of them are perfect for a drink or simple meal while you're waiting for your bus to Eze-sur-Mer or back to Nice.

RESTAURANTS

The best restaurants in Eze are those attached to the luxury hotels that cling to the hillside – see under Accommodation. Lunch at one of these need not break the bank, if you are content to choose from one of the set menus; dinner is always a leisurely gourmet affair and priced accordingly. For the more modest end of the scale, head for the place de la Collette at the base of the citadel.

● *It may be touristy, but Eze has genuine charm*

Le Bélèze € Offers wider-ranging choice of dishes than many of the other restaurants in this area. ❸ pl. de la Collette. ❶ 04 93 41 19 09.

Cheval Blanc € Slightly better value than some of its companions; menu is mainly pizza, standard Italian dishes and salads.
❸ pl. de la Collette. ❶ 04 93 41 03 17.

Auberge de Troubadour €€ In contrast to the haute cuisine of the château hotels and the mass-market offerings of the budget restaurants, this rustic establishment serves authentic and traditional Provençal fare. ❸ 4 rue du Brec. ❶ 04 93 41 19 03.
❶ Tues–Sat lunch and dinner, Mon dinner only. Closed Sun and in the first week of Jul.

Château Eza €€–€€€ Award-winning cuisine from chef Laurent Le Cann includes two lunchtime *menus saveurs* that are reasonably priced considering their outstanding quality, and a choice of light meals in the afternoon ❸ rue de la Pise. ❶ 04 93 41 12 24.
❶ www.chateaueza.com ❶ 12.00–15.00 (lunch), 15.00–17.30 (tapas and salads only); 19.30–22.00 (dinner).

Château de la Chèvre d'Or €€€ Opinions vary on whether this or the Château Eza is Eze's leader in the restaurant stakes, but Philippe Labbé's handling of Mediterranean cuisine has many fans.
❸ rue du Barri. ❶ 04 92 10 66 66. ❶ www.chevredor.com
❶ Daily for lunch and dinner, except Nov–early Mar.

ACCOMMODATION

Eze's popularity with the rich and famous has given it some of the most luxurious hotels on the Côte d'Azur. However, cheaper accommodation can be found in the area, including B&Bs and gîtes, if you don't mind staying a little way from the old town. The tourist office can provide a comprehensive list of all the options. A car is essential if you want to use Eze as a base for extensive sightseeing on the Riviera, though.

Auberge du Soleil € This villa-style accommodation on the Basse Corniche in Eze-sur-Mer is very close to the sea and has 10 comfortable en-suite guest rooms. The good on-site restaurant makes half-board a reasonable option. 📍 44 av. Liberté.
📞 04 93 01 51 46.

La Bastide aux Camélias €€ A charming, four-roomed B&B with swimming pool, sauna and gardens, just outside Eze village. 📍 3C route de l'Adret. 📞 04 93 41 13 68. 🌐 www.bastideauxcamelias.com

Château de la Chèvre d'Or €€€ The 24-room Relais & Châteaux hotel, a conversion of several medieval houses in the old town, has hosted many celebrity visitors, including Walt Disney, a frequent guest here. In addition to two swimming pools, stunning views and all the usual top-flight facilities, it boasts three restaurants: the grill room, the 'traditional' dining room and a summertime terrace restaurant.
📍 rue du Barri. 📞 04 92 10 66 66. 🌐 www.chevredor.com

Château Eza €€€ The former home of Prince William of Sweden and only relatively recently converted to a hotel, this fashionable clifftop residence has just 10 rooms, combining an authentic medieval setting with all modern facilities and unmatchable views over the sea.
📍 rue de la Pise. 📞 04 93 41 12 24. 🌐 www.chateaueza.com

St-Paul-de-Vence

St-Paul is another fortified hilltop village beloved of artists, tourists and celebrities. Lying to the west of Nice and some way inland, it doesn't have the sea views of Eze but the old village inside the medieval walls is rather larger, and the streets a little wider, so that even though it becomes equally busy in the summer it feels a little less crowded. It also possesses an extra major attraction in the shape of the Fondation Maeght, one of the world's most important collections of modern art, contained in a purpose-built gallery set in an attractive hillside garden.

St-Paul-de-Vence was an important enough town in the Middle Ages to be fortified by the Kings of France, but by the beginning of the 20th century had become a rural backwater. After World War I it attracted the attention of some of the most illustrious artists of the time, including Picasso, Modigliani, Matisse, Braque and Dufy, all of whom paid for lodging at the (then) humble inn of the Colombe d'Or with paintings, many of which still hang there. From these beginnings it became a centre of modern art and art dealers and latterly a major tourist destination.

GETTING THERE

The TAM bus 400 departs from quai 5 in Nice's central bus station approximately hourly every day, including public holidays; it can also be boarded on the prom. des Anglais. The journey to St-Paul-de-Vence takes about 45 mins, passing through Cagnes (about 30 mins from Nice) and continuing on to the town of Vence (about 1 hour from Nice). Ligne d'Azur no. 94 will take you to Vence and Cagnes but bypasses St-Paul.

Away from the main shopping streets you can have St Paul to yourself

The bus to St-Paul also leads past the resort town of Cagnes-sur-Mer and continues to Vence, both worthy destinations in their own right; it is possible to combine a half-day in St-Paul with a visit to either of these (to do all three in a day would be stretching it).

You can also catch a train from Nice-Ville station to Cagnes but not the other two destinations.

SIGHTS

The bus stops outside the tiny medieval Chapelle de Ste-Claire on the main road. From there it is a short walk past the Colombe d'Or, now a luxury hotel rather than the humble inn of yesteryear, into the place de Gaulle. On your right is the large *boules* pitch, which hosts regional tournaments and celebrity matches from time to time. At the far end of the place de Gaulle you come to the main gate of the fortified town, from which leads the principal street, rue Grande. If the street is already a little crowded, it's better to carry on past the main gate and make a complete circuit of the ramparts, which holds great views over the countryside in all directions. At various intervals you can dive into the town through the narrow connecting streets.

Despite the numbers of visitors, and the obvious commercialisation which has turned almost every ancient house into an art gallery or purveyor of designer chocolates and olive oils, the maze of flower-bedecked streets retains an irresistible charm. Halfway along, rue Grande opens out to accommodate the Grande Fontaine of 1850, for a long time the town's main water supply (always a problem in the mountains) – the water is not drinkable now. The Eglise Collégiale, the church at the top of the old town, dates from the 13th century and has an atmospheric interior combining medieval and baroque elements. Facing it across the square is the *Mairie* or town hall, occupying the 12th-century keep of the original castle; next door is the town's museum, the Musée d'Histoire Locale (🕐 daily 10.00–12.30, 13.30–17.30). At the far end of the rue Grande and through the porte de Nice which cuts through the ramparts lies the town cemetery, which contains the grave of Marc Chagall (see page 100), who died here in 1984.

Office de Tourisme The small but very helpful tourist office just inside the main gate of the town has good maps and brochures on accommodation and shopping, and offers guided tours; they also rent out sets of *boules* for a game on St-Paul's famous pitch and even sell an instruction package to introduce you to the game.

📍 2 rue Grande. 📞 04 93 32 86 95. 🌐 www.saint-pauldevence.com

Fondation Marght

This world-class art gallery is a stiff 20-minute uphill walk from near the bus stop at Chapelle Ste-Claire. If you have your own car it's not a

🔽 *At the Fondation Maeght the garden is an art gallery, too*

problem to drive up and use the car park at the gallery; otherwise, older and less agile visitors might find the trek difficult and would be well advised to take a taxi from the stand near the Colombe d'Or.

Aimé Maeght came to the south of France as a Belgian war orphan in 1914 and later opened an art gallery in Cannes. He and his wife Marguerite became friends of most of the leading exponents of art in the inter-war years in France, including Bonnard, Matisse, Braque, Miró, Calder and Giacometti, and through their other gallery in Paris helped to promote their work. In 1964 they set up a private foundation to which they donated their own extensive collection, and the Fondation now owns more than 9000 works by world-famous modern artists. The striking modern gallery was designed by Catalan architect Josep Luis Sert, and the surrounding garden is decorated with typically quirky figures by Joan Miró and Giacometti. There is no set route through the gallery and no particular plan of arrangement of the ever-changing exhibits, all of which makes the experience one of personal discovery rather than art education.

ⓐ Montée des Trious, St-Paul-de-Vence. ☎ 04 93 32 81 63.
ⓦ www.maeght.com ⏱ Daily 10.00–19.00 July–Sept; 10.00–12.30, 14.30–18.00 Oct–June. Admission charge (with extra charge if you want to take photographs).

RETAIL THERAPY

If you are seriously contemplating acquiring an original work of art then you could spend a day in the commercial galleries of St-Paul. Another strength of the town's shops is furniture, ceramics and other objects of interior design, and other boutiques specialise in figurines,

● *There's plenty to tempt the shopper in St-Paul-de-Vence*

traditional garments and other gifts with a Provençal air. The accent is mostly on authentic, quality goods at a commensurate price, rather than cheap souvenirs, so if you're are seriously shopping, bring your credit card! The tourist office issues a comprehensive catalogue of local shops to help you find what you're looking for.

There is a Provençal produce market near the *boules* arena at the entrance to the town on Tues–Thur and Sat.

CAFES & RESTAURANTS

Fine food at fine prices is not hard to come by in the restaurants of the luxury hotels which surround St-Paul. Luckily there's also no shortage of simpler establishments good for a morning coffee, cooling drink or simple lunch.

Dolce Italia € If you have made the climb up the steps to the church you're probably ready for one of the true Italian cappuccinos or ice creams that this café specialises in. ⓐ 13 pl. de l'Eglise. ❶ 04 93 24 09 95. ⓛ Daily.

Malabar € Calling itself a 'gourmet snack bar', this café on the ramparts serves good-value sandwiches, *pissaladière* and other snacks, and lunches, all to take away or eat on the spot.
ⓐ Remparts Ouest. ❶ 04 93 32 60 14. ⓛ Daily 11.00–18.00.

Le Tilleul Menthe €–€€ This busy terrace restaurant is just inside the walls to the left of the town gate. The food is unsophisticated but tasty and service is efficient. In summer it attracts wandering entertainers – children will love it. ⓐ impasse Muriers. ❶ 04 93 32 80 36. ⓛ Daily for lunch and dinner.

Le Saint Paul €€€ Mediterranean food doesn't come any better than the Michelin-starred cuisine on the flowery terrace of this Relais & Château hotel.

EVENTS

The local tourist authority works hard to make sure its visitors don't become bored, with a full programme of events ranging from summer concerts to the folk festival Fête Patronale de Ste-Claire, three days of traditional costumes, dancing and processions at the beginning of August. This is followed closely by four days of *pétanque* competitions that attract devotees of the *boules* from as far afield as Japan. Autumn sees a heritage weekend in September and the annual festival of the local wine harvest in October. The tourist office issues good seasonal lists of all the organised activities in St-Paul.

ACTIVITIES

St-Paul is a good centre for walking in the surrounding hills, with waymarked trails leading from near the Chapelle Ste-Claire on the main road. If you've never played *pétanque*, you can learn from a local on the town's famous arena with one of the instruction packages from the tourist office.

ACCOMMODATION

St-Paul, like Eze (see pages 130–131) has plenty of luxury accommodation to suit its celebrity visitors. More cost-wise travellers will find lodgings further out of town, but if you're not travelling by car it doesn't matter too much, as most are close to the main bus route.

Hostellerie les Remparts €–€€ One of the few hotels right in the middle of the old town, this traditional stone-built house, with 9 guest rooms and a good regional restaurant, offers a warm welcome. 72 rue Grande, St-Paul-de-Vence. ❶ 04 93 32 09 88.

Hotel le Hameau €€ Within walking distance of the town and the Fondation Maeght, this charming hotel has 17 comfortable rooms and a large swimming pool – and the breakfast marmalade is made with oranges grown on the premises. ❶ 528 route de la Colle, St-Paul-de-Vence. ❶ 04 93 32 80 24. Ⓦ www.le-hameau.com

Les Vergers de Saint Paul €€–€€€ The 15 rooms and 2 suites are grouped in a two-storey and a one-storey building around the large central swimming pool. The secluded location is less than 1 km (1/2 mile) from the town. ❶ route de la Colle, St-Paul-de-Vence. ❶ 04 93 32 94 24. Ⓦ www.hotel-vergers-saint-paul.cote.azur.fr

La Colombe d'Or €€€ What was a simple country inn at the time the artists descended on St-Paul has become a destination hotel and restaurant that is proud of its celebrity guests and the works of art that decorate the place (donated in lieu of payment by the likes of Modigliani and Picasso). It's fair to point out that while some guests and diners have raved about La Colombe, others have found it noisy and unfriendly. ❶ pl. de Gaulle. ❶ 04 93 32 80 02. Ⓦ www.la-colombe-dor.com ❶ Closed Nov–beginning of Christmas season.

---

❶ *Gare Nice-Ville is the rail hub of the Riviera*

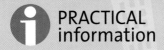

PRACTICAL
information

Directory

GETTING THERE
By air
Nice-Côte d'Azur airport serves flights from many UK and Irish airlines, including Aer Lingus (from Dublin and Cork), British Airways, British Midland and Bmibaby (from Birmingham and East Midlands), EasyJet (from London Gatwick, Luton and Stansted, Bristol, Liverpool, Newcastle and Belfast) and Globespan (from Edinburgh and Glasgow). Flight time from London is about 2 hours. Direct flights from other countries include Canada (Air Transat from Montréal) and USA (Air France, Delta from New York JFK).

By train
From the London Waterloo via Eurostar to Paris Gare du Nord and then by TGV from Paris Gare de Lyon to Nice-Ville averages about 11 hours, and return fares are cheaper than those of many low-cost airlines. If you are Inter-railing or Eurailing, you can reach Nice not only from cities in France but also by direct international trains. The monthly *Thomas Cook European Rail Timetable* has up-to-date schedules for European international and national train services.

Eurostar reservations (UK) ☎ 08705 186 186. 🌐 www.eurostar.com

Thomas Cook European Rail Timetable ☎ (UK) 01733 416477; (USA) 1 800 322 3834. 🌐 www.thomascookpublishing.com

By car
Driving from the UK via Calais will take you 2–3 days to cover the 1200km (720 miles) from Calais to Nice: head for Marseilles and pick

up the A8 *autoroute*, 'La Provençale', to Nice. For the approaches to Nice see page 52.

TRAVEL INSURANCE

Visitors from the UK are covered by EU reciprocal health schemes while in France. They require a European Health Insurance Card (EHIC). This will not cover all possible expenses, and only guarantees emergency treatment. Always make sure you have adequate travel insurance, covering not only health, but possessions, etc. All non EU travellers should ensure they have adequate insurance before they travel.

ENTRY FORMALITIES

Documentation

Passports are needed by UK visitors and all others except EU citizens who can produce a national identity card. Visits of up to three months do not require a visa if your nationality is UK, Republic of Ireland, US, Canadian, Australian or New Zealand. Other travellers should consult the French embassy or tourist office in their own country on visa requirements.

ⓦ www.diplomatie.gouv.fr/venir/visas/index.html

Customs

Residents of the UK, Ireland and other EU countries may bring into France personal possessions and goods for personal use, including a reasonable amount of tobacco and alcohol, provided they have been bought in the EU. There are few formalities at the point of entry into France. Residents of non-EU countries, and EU residents arriving from a non-EU country, may bring in up to 400 cigarettes and 50 cigars or 50g (2 oz) tobacco; 2 litres (3 bottles) of wine and 1 litre

(approx. 2 pints) of spirits or liqueurs. The full regulations and definitions of 'reasonable amount' may be checked at
Ⓦ www.douane.gouv.fr

MONEY

The euro (€)is the official currency in France. €1 = 100 cents. It comes in notes of €5, €10, €20, €50, €100, €200 and €500. Coins are in denominations of €1 and €2, and 1, 2, 5, 10, 20 and 50 cents.

ATM machines can be found at the airport, railway stations, shopping centres and outside most banks, and they accept most British and international debit and credit cards. They are the quickest and most convenient way to obtain cash. Instructions on use are available in English and other major European languages.

The most widely accepted credit cards are VISA and Mastercard, though other major credit cards such as American Express are also commonly accepted in restaurants and shops. Traveller's cheques and foreign money can be cashed at most banks, and bureaux de change, in Nice – you may have to produce your passport or other ID.

American Express operate a 7 day a week bureau de change. ⓐ 11 prom. des Anglais. ① 04 93 16 53 53. ◐ 09.00–20.00 Oct–Apr; 09.00–21.00 May–Sept; 10.00–18.00 on public holidays.

HEALTH, SAFETY & CRIME

Tap water is safe (if not it is marked *eau non potable*, not for drinking) but the French and most visitors prefer to consume one of the many brands of mineral water.

Medical facilities in France are of an excellent standard, but expensive – ensure you have adequate travel insurance. Most minor ailments can be taken to pharmacies, indicated by a green cross sign – the one in the rue Masséna pedestrian zone is 24-hour. Pharmacies have expert staff who are qualified to offer medical advice and dispense a wide range of medicines. Many drugs, such as aspirin, that are widely available in the UK are obtainable only at pharmacies in France.

Nice is a safe city, by and large. The beach and the streets west and north of the promenade des Anglais are not the best places to be late at night (and budget travellers should never be tempted to sleep overnight on the beach to save on accommodation). Otherwise, take normal sensible precautions – avoid deserted streets by night, keep valuables secure from pickpockets and

⬢ *Rue Masséna's pharmacy is always open*

opportunist bag-snatchers by day. Never leave valuables in a car, as theft from (and of) automobiles is one of Nice's main crime issues. You may encounter one of the hustlers who especially frequent the seafront. A common scam is to 'give' you a worthless ring or trinket and then as the conversation drags on ask for payment of 'whatever you think it is worth'. There are also plausible 'distressed tourists' around – some quite elderly – who will spin you a heartbreaking story of being suddenly penniless and not being able even to phone their consulate. In both cases, simply walking away is normally sufficient to deter the scam operators. Public disorder and drunkenness are rare – so rare that people stand and stare at the occasional drunks.

There is a mobile police post in the rue Masséna and regular but low-profile patrols in the main tourist areas. In general the police are approachable and helpful, though not guaranteed to speak English. In Nice itself the Police Municipale are the police most in evidence and oversee traffic and petty crime; the Police Nationale deal with more serious matters. Lost property and minor theft should be reported to the Police Municipale, anything more serious to the Police Nationale. In country districts and on motorways the (usually armed) Gendarmerie Nationale are the main law enforcement body.

Commissariat Central de Police (Central Police Station) @ 1 av. Maréchal Foch. ☎ 04 92 17 22 22. ◷ 24 hours a day. Interpreters are available 08.00–12.00, 14.00–18.00, and on ☎ 04 92 17 20 31.

Police Municipale (Lost property office) @ 1 rue de la Terrasse. ☎ 04 97 13 44 00. ◷ 08.30–17.00 Mon–Thur, 08.30–15.45 Fri.

OPENING HOURS

Shops Generally 09.00–12.00, 14.00–19.00 Mon–Sat (those on the main pedestrian areas tend to stay open later and don't close for lunch).

Banks 08.30–12.00, 13.30–17.00 Mon–Fri.

Some museums are closed on Mon.

TOILETS

Museums generally have good toilet facilities – connoisseurs of such things will find the hi-tech facilities in the Fondation Maeght (see page 135) particularly impressive. The average café and restaurant toilet is clean but small and often unisex; the better the establishment the better the facilities. Public toilets in Nice are the modern, hygienic coin-operated cubicles (which young children shouldn't be allowed to use unaccompanied).

CHILDREN

The only health threat to children on the Riviera is the strength of the sun – ensure that they have adequate protection from it at all times. If you are travelling with babies or young children you can buy nappies, baby food and other supplies in supermarkets and pharmacies. Restaurants are used to children eating with the family, and junior menus and smaller portions are commonly offered. Many attractions and transport providers have reduced rates for children. There is plenty to keep the kids entertained in Nice and on the Riviera generally. Here's just a small selection:

- The sea and the beaches – the sandy beaches of Villefranche and Cap-Ferrat in particular.

- A ride on the *petit train touristique* (see page 42).

- The carousel in the Jardin Albert 1er facing the seafront, and the 'human statue' street entertainers in the rue Masséna pedestrian area (though perhaps a bit scary for the very young).

- Cap Ferrat's zoo (see page 115).

- The playground on top of the Château hill. There is also a puppet show on the main esplanade of the Château every Sunday afternoon, 16.00–17.00.

○ *Simple fun for the kids in Jardin Albert 1er*

- **Le Castel des Deux Rois** mini-amusement park at in eastern Nice, between the port and Terra Amata (see page 101) has its own *petit train*, mini-golf, giant chessboard, wooden play huts and more.

- **Marineland: Parc de la Mer et de l'Aventure** This theme park is just a short train ride away near Antibes. In addition to the Wild West area, an aquasplash and adventure golf, the family can enjoy performing dolphins that can be petted, a pirate ship that lets you get close up to orcas, a scary shark tunnel and a tropical aquarium ⓐ Off the N7 highway nr Antibes. ⓣ 04 93 33 49 49. ⓦ www.marineland.fr ⓛ Daily 10.00–22.30, Jun–Sept. ⓝ Frequent trains from Nice-Ville take about 25 mins to Biot station, about 2 mins on foot from the park.

COMMUNICATIONS

Phones

The area code for south-east France is 04, followed by a number which is always 8 digits. When dialling from anywhere within France, dial all 10 digits, including the 04. To call Nice numbers from outside France, dial your own international prefix (00 in most countries) followed by 33 4 followed by the local 8-digit number. Calling from France to abroad: Dial 00 for an international connection, followed by your country code (UK 44, Republic of Ireland 353, USA and Canada 1, Australia 61, New Zealand 64, South Africa 27) and then the area code (leaving out the first '0' if there is one) and the number. Card-operated public phone booths are everywhere, and you can make international calls from them. You can buy phone cards (*télécartes*) at *tabacs* (newsagent/tobacconist shops sporting a red diamond sign outside), post offices and some cafés and rail stations.

Post

Post offices can be found all over Nice – the most central ones are in the rue Gassin in the old town and on av. Jean Médecin just south of blvd Victor Hugo. They open 09.00–19.00 on weekdays and some close 12.00–14.00. They are also closed on Sat afternoons and all day Sun. Stamps can be bought there or at *tabacs*. Postcards to the UK and Ireland will normally arrive in 2–3 days, taking a little longer to non-European destinations. Current rates for sending postcards are Europe €0.50, North America €0.90, Australia and New Zealand €0.90.

● *France has a modern and efficient postal service*

Internet

Even some smaller hotels may provide an internet connection, but in any case internet cafés are plentiful in Nice. One of the most central is just off the prom. des Anglais:

Nemeos 🄰 2 rue Halévy. 🅣 04 93 87 37 48. 🄴 contact@nemeos.com 🄲 Daily 10.00–22.00 (24.00 Fri and Sat).

ELECTRICITY

France runs on 220v with 2-pin plugs. British appliances will need a simple adaptor, easily obtained at any electrical or hardware store in the centre of Nice. US and other equipment designed for 110v will need a transformer (*transformateur*).

FURTHER INFORMATION

Tourist offices

The Nice Convention and Visitors Bureau maintains three offices, on the seafront and at the airport and the rail station. They stock a wide range of literature and maps and have helpful staff who can make accommodation bookings and sell tickets for many attractions and events, including Carnaval.

Office du Tourisme et des Congrès 🄰 5 prom. des Anglais. 🅣 0892 70 74 07. 🅕 04 92 14 48 03. 🄲 08.00–20.00 Mon–Sat, Jun–Sept; 09.00–18.00 Mon–Sat, Oct–May and on all Sun throughout the year.

Office du Tourisme et des Congrès 🄰 Nice Côte d'Azur Airport– Terminal 1. 🅣 0892 70 74 07. 🅕 04 93 21 44 50. 🄲 08.00–21.00, daily in Jun–Sept and Mon–Sat in Oct–May.

Office du Tourisme et des Congrès

🅐 Gare Nice-Ville, av. Thiers.

🅣 0892 70 74 07. 🅕 04 93 16 85 16.

🅛 08.00–20.00 Mon–Sat, 09.00–19.00 Sun, Jun–Sept; 08.00–19.00 Mon–Sat, 09.00–18.00 Sun, Oct–May.

Centre Régional Information Jeunesse Côte d'Azur is an advice and information centre for young independent travellers in eastern central Nice, well-signposted from the middle of town.

🅐 19 rue Gioffredo. 🅣 04 93 80 93 93, 🅕 04 93 80 30 33.

🅛 08.45–18.45 Mon–Fri.

Websites

The Nice tourist office website is very informative and includes a comprehensive instant accommodation booking service.

Ⓦ www.nicetourism.com

Additional information and listings, especially of events, can be found on the city council website. Ⓦ www.nice.fr

Other useful sites include:

Ⓦ www.guideriviera.com (the official site of the entire Riviera)

Ⓦ www.cotedazur-en-fetes.com (events on the Riviera)

Ⓦ http://riviera.angloinfo.com (English-speaking services and information).

If you're trying to track down a business of any sort, use the French Yellow Pages site at Ⓦ www.pagesjaunes.fr, which also provides location maps for all its listings.

MEDIA & LISTINGS

The free paper *La Strada*, available at the tourist office, gives a good round-up of happenings in Nice and all along the Côte d'Azur, in French. *Nice*, published by the municipality and distributed in hotels, also in French, is a more general but topical magazine for visitors.

As you would expect given the expatriate heritage, the Nice region has a couple of English-language newspapers, *The Riviera Reporter* and *The Riviera Times*, available from the bigger newsagents in the centre of town (where you can also buy UK, US and other foreign newspapers).

TRAVELLERS WITH DISABILITIES

The bigger installations, such as the airport and central rail station, and many of the larger hotels, have access and facilities adapted for visitors with mobility problems. All road crossings in Nice are wheelchair-accessible, as is the central section of the beach, accessed from opposite the Jardin Albert 1er. Elsewhere the position is less satisfactory, and the steep hills and narrow, cobbled streets of Eze and St-Paul, for instance, are unsuited to wheelchair-based tourists. Useful organisations for advice and information include:

RADAR The principal UK forum and pressure group for people with disabilities. **a** 12 City Forum, 250 City Road, London EC1V 8AF. **t** (020) 7250 3222. **w** www.radar.org.uk

SATH (Society for Accessible Travel & Hospitality) advises US-based travellers with disabilities. **a** 347 Fifth Ave, Suite 610, New York, NY 10016. **t** (212) 447 7284. **f** (212) 725 8253 **w** www.sath.org

Association des Paralysés de France Délégation Départementale des Alpes Maritimes. **a** 21, blvd Mantéga-Righi, Nice. **t** 04 92 15 78 70.

Useful phrases

Although English is widely spoken in Nice, these words and phrases may come in handy. See also the phrases for specific situations in other parts of the book.

English	French	Approx. pronunciation
BASICS		
Yes	Oui	Wee
No	Non	Nawng
Please	S'il vous plaît	Seel voo pleh
Thank you	Merci	Mehrsee
Hello	Bonjour	Bawngzhoor
Goodbye	Au revoir	Aw revwahr
Excuse me	Excusez-moi	Ekskeweh mwah
Sorry	Désolé(e)	Dehzoleh
That's okay	Ça va	Sahr vahr
To	À	Ah
From	De	Der
I don't speak French	Je ne parle pas français	Zher ner pahrl pah frahngsay
Do you speak English	Vous parlez anglais?	Voopahrlay ahnglay?
Good morning	Bonjour	Bawng-zhoor
Good afternoon	Bonjour	Bawng-zhoor
Good evening	Bonsoir	Bawng-swah
Goodnight	Bonne nuit	Bun nwee
My name is ...	Je m'appelle...	Zher mahpehl ...
DAYS & TIMES		
Monday	Lundi	Langdee
Tuesday	Mardi	Mahrdee
Wednesday	Mercredi	Mehrkrerdee
Thursday	Jeudi	Zhurdee
Friday	Vendredi	Vahndrerdee
Saturday	Samedi	Sahmdee
Sunday	Dimanche	Deemahngsh
Morning	Le matin	Ler mahtang
Afternoon	L'après-midi	Lahpreh meedee
Evening	Le soir	Ler swahr
Night	La nuit	Lah nwee
Yesterday	Hier	Yehr

English	French	Approx. pronunciation
Today	Aujourd'hui	Ojoordewee
Tomorrow	Demain	Dermang
What time is it?	Quelle heure est-il?	Kel urr ehteel?
It is ...	Il est...	Eel eh ...
09.00	Neuf heures	Nurv urr
Midday	Midi	Meedee
Midnight	Minuit	Meenurhee

NUMBERS

English	French	Approx. pronunciation
One	Un/Une	Ang/Ewn
Two	Deux	Dur
Three	Trois	Trwah
Four	Quatre	Kahtr
Five	Cinq	Sangk
Six	Six	Seess
Seven	Sept	Seht
Eight	Huit	Weet
Nine	Neuf	Nurf
Ten	Dix	Deess
Eleven	Onze	Awngz
Twelve	Douze	Dooz
Twenty	Vingt	Vang
Fifty	Cinquante	Sangkahnt
One hundred	Cent	Sahng

MONEY

English	French	Approx. pronunciation
I would like to change these traveller's cheques/this currency	J'aimerais changer ces chèques de voyage/ ces devises	Zhaymray shahngzheh seh shek der vwahahzh/ seh derveez
Where is the nearest ATM?	Où se trouve le distributeur de billets le plus proche?	Oo ser troov ler distribewter der beeyeh ler plew prosh?
Do you accept credit cards?	Vous acceptez les cartes de crédit?	Voos aksepteh leh kart der krehdee?

SIGNS & NOTICES

English	French	Approx. pronunciation
Airport	Aéroport	Ahehrohpohr
Rail station/Platform	Gare/Quai	Gahr/Kay
Smoking/non-smoking	Fumeurs/non fumeurs	Fewmurh/nawng fewmurh
Toilets	Toilettes	Twahlayt
Ladies/Gentlemen	Femmes/Hommes	Fam/Ommh
Subway	Métro	Maytroa

Emergencies

EMERGENCY NUMBERS
The following are all national free emergency numbers:
Medical/ambulance (SAMU) 15.
Police/Gendarmerie 17.
Fire (Sapeurs-Pompiers) 18.
Any emergency service 112. This is also the number that *must* be used when calling from mobile phones.
Nice Central Police Station ❶ 04 92 17 22 22. (Nice Central Police has a tourist department where interpreters are available).
❶ 04 92 17 20 31. ◔ Daily 08.00–12.00, 14.00–16.30.

MEDICAL SERVICES
Night pharmacy ❸ 7 rue Masséna. ❶ 04 93 87 78 94.
Hôpital St–Roch Hospital with 24-hour emergency services.
❸ Entrance on 5 rue Pierre Devoluy. ❶ 04 92 03 33 75.
Hôpital Lenval Specialising in child health emergencies.
❸ 57 av. de la Californie. ❶ 04 92 03 03 03.
Riviera Medical Services: English-speaking doctors on call (not necessarily for emergencies). ❶ 04 93 26 12 70.
SOS Dentaire Emergency dental care at night and on Sundays and public holidays. ❶ 04 93 76 53 53; 04 92 13 00 99.

CONSULATES & EMBASSIES
Australia Embassy. ❸ 4 rue Jean Rey, Paris. ❶ 01 40 59 33 00.
Canada Consulate. ❸ 10 rue Lamartine, Nice. ❶ 04 93 92 93 22.
❶ 04 93 92 55 51.
New Zealand Embassy. ❸ 7 rue Léonard da Vinci, Paris.
❶ 01 45 01 43 43.

EMERGENCIES

Republic of Ireland Consulate. 🏠 152 blvd J-F Kennedy, Cap d'Antibes. 📞 04 93 61 50 63.

South Africa Embassy. 🏠 59 quai d'Orsay, Paris. 📞 01 53 59 23 23.

UK Consulate General. 🏠 24 av. du Prado, Marseille. 📞 04 91 15 72 10.

USA Consulate. 🏠 7 av. Gustave V, 3rd Floor, Nice. 📞 04 93 88 89 55. 📞 04 93 87 07 38.

🔺 *The Police Municipale is there to help you*

EMERGENCY PHRASES

Help! Au secours! *Ossercoor!*   **Fire!** Au feu! *Oh fur!*

Stop! Stop! *Stop!*

Call an ambulance/a doctor/the police/the fire service!
Appelez une ambulance/un médecin/la police/les pompiers!
Ahperleh ewn ahngbewlahngss/ang medesang/lah poleess/leh pompeeyeh!

ACKNOWLEDGEMENTS & FEEDBACK

The publishers would like to thank the following individuals and organisations for supplying their copyright photographs for this book.
A1 Pix: pages 5, 13, 42/43, 47, 71, 75, 83, 110/111, 113
Office du Tourisme et des Congrès, Nice: page 17
Ethel Davies: pages 117 & 129
Paul Medbourne & Patsy Trimnell: all other pages.

Proofreader: Angela Chevalier-Watts
Copy-editor: Stephen York

Send your thoughts to
books@thomascook.com

- Found a great bar, club, shop or must-see sight that we don't feature?

- Like to tip us off about any information that needs a little updating?

- Want to tell us what you love about this handy little guidebook and more importantly how we can make it even handier?

Then here's your chance to tell all! Send us ideas, discoveries and recommendations today and then look out for your valuable input in the next edition of this title. As an extra 'thank you' from Thomas Cook Publishing, you'll be automatically entered into our exciting monthly prize draw.

Email to the above address or write to:
CitySpots Project Editor, Thomas Cook Publishing, PO Box 227, Unit 15/16, Coningsby Road, Peterborough PE3 8SB, UK.